The Scientific Foundations of Jainism

LALA SUNDAR LAL JAIN RESEARCH SERIES

General Editor

PROF. SATYA RANJAN BANERJEE

Editorial Board

DR. PADMANABH S. JAINI **PROF. DAYANAND BHARGAVA**

PROF. W.B. BOLLEE **PROF. KLAUS BRUHN**

VOLUME V

The Scientific Foundations of Jainism

K.V. Mardia

MOTILAL BANARSIDASS PUBLISHERS
PRIVATE LIMITED • DELHI

First Edition: Delhi, 1990
Second Revised Edition: Delhi, 1996
Corrected Edition: 2002

ISBN: 81-208-0658-1 (Cloth)
ISBN: 81-208-0659-x (Paper)

Also available at:
MOTILAL BANARSIDASS
41 U.A. Bungalow Road, Jawahar Nagar, Delhi 110 007
8 Mahalaxmi Chambers, 22 Bhulabhai Desai Road, Mumbai 400 026
236, 9th Main III Block, Jayanagar, Bangalore 560 011
120 Royapettah High Road, Mylapore, Chennai 600 004
Sanas Plaza, 1302 Baji Rao Road, Pune 411 002
8 Camac Street, Kolkata 700 017
Ashok Rajpath, Patna 800 004
Chowk, Varanasi 221 001

Printed in India
BY JAINENDRA PRAKASH JAIN AT SHRI JAINENDRA PRESS,
A-45 NARAINA, PHASE-I, NEW DELHI 110 028
AND PUBLISHED BY NARENDRA PRAKASH JAIN FOR
MOTILAL BANARSIDASS PUBLISHERS PRIVATE LIMITED,
BUNGALOW ROAD, DELHI 110 007

In memory of my father

VARDICHANDJI

and of my mother

SANGARIBAI

"Science without religion is lame,
Religion without science is blind."

"....a person who is religiously enlightened appears to me to be one who has, to the best of his ability, liberated himself from the fetters of his selfish desires...."

Einstein (1940, 1941) see, p. 106

Jain = Person who has conquered himself.

FOREWORD

IT WAS VERY flattering to be asked by Professor Mardia to write a Foreword to his book *The Scientific Foundations of Jainism* and I am delighted to do so. I am pleased for a number of reasons. I have known Professor Mardia for a good number of years and we have had many interesting discussions on questions relating to Jainism. We did, in fact, discuss his intention to write an explanation of Jain philosophy and religion in terms of modern science: I am pleased that I saw the first draft of this book and I am delighted to be one of the first to read it in its final form. I believe that he has made a valuable contribution to the literature on Jainism. And, one other reason must be mentioned: perhaps some of the reflected glory will fall on me and the learnd and wise, reading Professor Mardia's book, will happen to glance at this modest note of mine!

Jainism is a religious system of great antiquity. Jain tradition traces its origins back through almost limitless time. Certainly the most sceptical cannot deny its nearly 3000 years of history. In that time, of course, it has not stood still. Generation after generation after generation of scholars have added and commented and explained, so that the total mass of written Jain scholarship is vast indeed, and growing vaster with every year that passes. I have always maintained, since I first began my own amateur study of Jainism, that its principles accord well with modern science. Jain thought, Jain philosophy is timeless. However, the ancient texts are written in the language of their particular time and their ideas are expressed in terms of the scientific vocabulary of their day. They are written in languages, Sanskrit and the Prakrits, which are well-adapted to give precision and clarity to abstruse and difficult ideas, though not infrequently they can be difficult of interpretation owing to extremes of terseness or of repetitiveness. The terminology can be difficult, and a modern book on any aspect of Jain thought will be littered with, and often rendered almost incomprehensible by, untranslated technical terms for which no concise modern equivalent has been sought or found.

Professor Mardia is a very distinguished scholar in a very exacting science. He is a mathematician, or more properly a statistician, and his university degrees include three doctorates. He is also a devoted and practising Jain. Thus he is particularly well-qualified to approach the task of rendering the basic principles and philosophy and ethics of Jainism in the terms of modern science. His book divides naturally into three parts. First he explains the basic ideas of the soul, karma, living beings and non-living matter, and brings these together in the Jain explanation of life and death and the universe. Next he moves from the general to the particular, to the practice of self-conquest and the path of the individual soul towards purification. Thirdly, in two chapters which demand, and reward, close reading, he places Jain logic in its rightful position as a valid and acceptable system, and draws together the most fundamental and up-to-date aspects of modern physics with the scientific theories of the Jain writers.

It is a great pleasure to me to see this work of Professor Mardia in its final form after the many years labour which he has put into it. It will, I am sure, be of value both to Jains living in the modern world who often find it difficult to discern the relevance of the writings of long-dead authors to the world today. It will also be of value to non-Jains, particularly those who approach the study of a little-known religion in a spirit of rational inquiry. This is, as I said earlier, an important contribution to the literature of Jainism. I congratulate Professor Mardia on his achievement and commend the book wholeheartedly to its readers.

PAUL MARETT
Loughborough University

PREFACE TO THE SECOND EDITION

IT IS REALLY gratifying to note that the first edition was well received by a large audience throughout the world. It has been most popular in the USA and the UK. This book has been successfully tried on the young generation and also it is a text book for a degree course at the De Montfort University, UK. With the increasing awareness of Jainism in the West, we expect this trend of understanding its scientific aspects to continue.

In addition to carrying out corrections in this revised edition, various definitions have been sharpened. Furthermore, Chapter 9, on Jain Logic, has been expanded, keeping in mind the increasing emphasis on the topic of Science and Truth. Further, we have added an Epilogue which highlights the main ideas of the book for the younger generation; this presentation has been well received as a single seminar. Also, the bibliography has been updated. There have been many important publications since the first edition. Namely, there has appeared various books related to Science and Jainism, e.g. Amrendravijay (1993), Jain, L.C. (1992), Jain, N.L. (1993) and Nandighoshvijay (1995). An excellent new basic text book for young children is by Kapashi et. al. (1994). Furthermore, there is a new translation of *Tattvārtha-sūtra* (Tatia, 1994) — the first English translation published outside India. The translation is elegant, simple, authentic and lucid together with important diagrams, tables and appendices. Another publication of great importance is *The Jain Declaration on Nature* (Singhvi, 1990) which was presented to His Royal Highness Prince Philip, President of the World Wide Fund for Nature. (The author has had the great privilege of contributing to both these projects.) These are also taken into account in the revised edition. My gratitude is owed to various encouraging reviewers, including Professor C.R. Rao, FRS (*The Jain*), Paul Marett (*Jain Journal, The Jain*), Krisiti L. Wiley (*Jain Mañjari*), Nemichand Jain (*Tirthankar*) and E.R. Sreekrishna Sarma (*The Adyar Library Bulletin*).

In particular, I am grateful to Dr. N.L. Jain who contributed substantially to this revision. My thanks are also due to Shri Chitrabhanu, Dr. Dulichand Jain and Raj Khullar for their constant encouragement, and to Harry Trickett for his comments. The members of the Yorkshire Jain Foundation have also contributed to the revisions through the regular readings of the book in their sessions. In particular, I benefited greatly from the comments of my wife Pavan, and my family members Bela, Raghu; Hemant, Preeti; and Neeta, Hemansu. Also, Pavan kindly proof read this edition and prepared the new index.

I am sure that the readers will be pleased that this edition is produced on better quality paper so enhancing the quality of the illustrations.

Micchā mi dukkaḍam

25th August, 1995; Paryūṣaṇa K.V. MARDIA

PREFACE

THERE HAS recently been a revival in seeking to understand Jainism and to search for its meaning in a modern context. Young Jains abroad who are brought up in a multicultural community are trying to understand its relevance in the new environment. Jainism, I suggest, was founded on scientific principles which can be assessed by each individual and to begin with, I have constructed four Axioms (fundamental basic assumptions) on which, in my opinion, Jainism is founded. These Axioms focus on the essence rather than on the detail.

This work started with my Inaugural Address as Professor of Statistics at the University of Leeds in 1975 where its relevance to Statistics was demonstrated. The Axioms were first presented to a small gathering in Leicester in 1979 which included Dr. Natubhai Shah and Paul Marett, when it received enthusiastic welcome. The book *The Jaina Path of Purification* (1979) by Professor Padmanabh S. Jaini of the University of California at Berkeley, rekindled my interest. The present book owes a great deal to Professor Jaini's work. The sources from the Jain scriptures which underly the following discussion can, in most cases be found in his book and, therefore, they have not been duplicated here. The spelling of Jain terms generally follows Professor Jaini's transliteration. His book also provides a very good glossary which will help the reader to realise that, for example, the words *karma* and *yoga* have completely different meanings in Jainism from those in Hinduism. That is, their popular meaning in English is not applicable (see the key words which follow). As a first introduction to the subject, we refer the reader to Paul Marett's book *Jainism Explained* (1985) and Vinod Kapashi's book *Jainism for Young Persons* (1985). A recent article by Ursula King (1987) is also recommended.

For this book we assume a nodding acquaintance with Mathematics and Physics. This allows us to use a sharper scientific and pictorial representation than would have otherwise been possible. Many Jain children follow their religion by birth rather than by conviction; there are about 9 million Jains in India and about 100,000 abroad. It is hoped that such a book as this might help teenagers to be Jains through conviction.

Chapter 1 gives a brief introduction to Jainism and lists four Axioms. Chapters 2 to 7 introduce the Axioms and discuss their plausibility in a modern context. Certain important details arise because of these assumptions and these are elaborated on. Chapter 8 outlines basic practices and Chapter 9 gives some ideas in Jain logic. Chapter 10 indicates how Jainism and Modern Science are related. Each chapter ends with the original terms with diacritical marks and our English equivalent; this will help the reader who wants to know the equivalence used as well as the diacritical spelling.

Appendix 1 gives the life of Mahavira as an individual. Appendix 2 gives some idea of the canonical scriptures from which the Axioms have been abstracted. Jainism does not have a single text like the Christian Bible; the number of existing canonical scriptures (by Svetambara) is as high as 45. Appendix 3A gives the precise original sources on which the axioms are based. Also, some important quotations which have been cited in the text are given in Appendix 3B. The important concept of purification stages is explained in a simple game-type representation in Appendix 4. We include a bibliography and index.

Those who wish to gain an idea of Jainism directly from the scriptures are recommended to read the Tattvartha-sutra of Umasvati; English translations are available, see Bibliography. However, for a first reading they should not take that text's comprehensive classification, sub-classification, etc. of Jainism too seriously, since this could sidetrack the reader from the essence into a mass of detail. These comprehensive synopses were essential for many centuries when the fundamentals were, in general, passed on by the word of mouth.

I wish to express my profound gratitude to Harry Trickett, who patiently went through the various drafts of the whole book and made many constructive comments. I also wish to acknowledge my gratitude to the President of Jain Samaj

Europe, Natubhai Shah, Professor P.S. Jaini, Gurudev Shree Chitrabhanu, Ganesh Lalwani, Paul Marett, Vinod Kapashi, Nigel Smeeton, Alan Watkins, Vijay Jain, Tim Hainsworth and also my dearest friend the late Kundan Jogator. I benefited greatly from the comments of my wife Pavan, my children Bela, Hemant and Neeta, and members of the Leeds Jain Group.

We have tried to re-interpret, as objectively as possible, various concepts in terms of modern science. One of the major difficulties in re-interpretation is that Jain terms are based on Prakrit/Sanskrit languages whereas modern science has its terminological roots in the Greek language. We recognise that in a small area of science, one works towards research degrees after many years of labour and one should expect similar dedication in order to understand the technical basis of Jainism. We should bear in mind the time taken to comprehend Albert Einstein's Theory of Relativity, even by experts. Finally, we should also stress the Jain claim that one can see the truth of Jain Science when one attains "Kevalajñāna" or infinite knowledge!

9th November, 1988, Diwali K.V. MARDIA

SPECIAL ACKNOWLEDGEMENT

MOST OF THE chapters have relied heavily on the basic material from Professor Padmanabh S. Jaini, *The Jaina Path of Purification* (1979), Berkeley University Press, Berkeley. (Reprinted by Motilal Banarsidass, Delhi, 1979.) In particular, I wish to acknowledge the excerpts cited in the text from the following pages of his book:

Chapter 1	p. 32
Chapter 3	p. 98
Chapter 4	pp. 109, 112-4, 125-7
Chapter 5	pp. 140-1, 147, 150
Chapter 6	pp. 159, 168-9, 171
Chapter 8	pp. 252-3

KEY WORDS

THE ORIGINAL TECHNICAL terms in Sanskrit and Prakrit have been appended to each chapter corresponding to our English translation. However, the following basic terms cannot be translated and are used frequently in the text. These should prove useful to those who are not acquainted with Jainism.

Jain:	noun: a person who follows Jainism; adjective: pertaining to Jainism, some prefer Jaina to Jain.
Digambara/Svetambara:	Two main Jain Schools having monks with no clothes and with white cotton garments respectively.
Karma/Karmic matter:	The matter determining the fate of the soul in rebirths. It is composed of (material) karmic particles (= *karmons*).
Mokṣa:	The state attained after emancipation from rebirths (= nirvāna).
Soul:	Pure sentient part with karmic matter.
Tirthankaras/Jinas:	The "Prophets" of Jainism; the omniscient spiritual teachers of Jainism.
Yoga:	The activities of body, mind and speech.

CONTENTS

Foreword *vii*
Preface to the Second Edition *ix*
Preface *xi*
Special Acknowledgement *xv*
Key Words *xvii*

CHAPTER 1: JAINS **1-8**
1.1 Introduction 1
1.2 Some characteristics of Jainism 4
1.3 Axiomatic approach 6
1.4 Glossary 8

CHAPTER 2: THEORY OF SOUL AND KARMIC MATTER (AXIOM 1) **9-19**
2.1 Axiom 9
2.2 The basic concepts 10
2.2.1 Soul 10
2.2.2 Karmons and karmic matter 10
2.2.3 Interaction 10
2.3 Terminology 11
2.3.1 Karmic process 11
2.3.2 Karmic density 13
2.3.3 Long-term equilibrium state 14
2.3.4 The nine reals 15
2.4 Important analogies 17
2.4.1 Magnetism 18
2.4.2 Miscellaneous analogies 18
2.5 Glossary 18

CHAPTER 3: HIERARCHY OF LIFE (AXIOM 2) **21-27**
3.1 The axiom 21
3.2 Life-units and life-axis 21
3.3 Division of the life axis according to the number of senses/intelligence 22

3.4 The four states of existence 25
3.5 Glossary 26

CHAPTER 4: CYCLES OF BIRTH AND DEATH (AXIOM 3) **29-42**
4.1 The axiom 29
4.2 The karmic components 29
4.3 What gets transported ? 32
4.4 Six existents 33
4.5 Jain particle physics 38
4.6 Practical implications of cycles 40
4.7 General comments 40
4.8 Glossary 41

CHAPTER 5: PRACTICAL KARMIC FUSION (AXIOM 4A) **43-51**
5.1 The axiom 43
5.2 Karmic components in practice 44
5.3 Volitional activities and the four passions 45
5.4 Degrees of passions 46
5.5 Glossary 51

CHAPTER 6: EXTREME ABSORPTION OF KARMONS (AXIOM 4B) **53-61**
6.1 The axiom 53
6.2 Implications 54
6.3 Volitional aspect of violence 56
6.4 The Jain universal temporal cycles 58
6.5 Glossary 60

CHAPTER 7: THE PATH TO SELF-CONQUEST (AXIOM 4C) **63-77**
7.1 The axiom 63
7.2 Purification axis and fourteen purification stages 64
7.3 First four stages 66
7.3.1 Definition of stages and internal motion 66
7.3.2 Description of the fourth stage and visible signs 67

7.4 Stage five to stage eleven 69
7.5 Levels twelve to fourteen 70
7.6 Schematic representations of the levels and transitions 71
7.7 Transitions between stages 75
7.8 Glossary 76

CHAPTER 8: THE PURIFICATION PRESCRIPTION **79-91**
8.1 Introduction 79
8.2 Eight qualities of True-Insight 79
8.3 Fifth stage for Jain laymen 80
8.4 Stage six and monks 81
8.5 The higher stages and meditation 83
8.6 The three jewels 85
8.7 Analogy of the spiritual progress with driving a car 87
8.8 Glossary 90

CHAPTER 9: JAIN LOGIC **93-100**
9.1 Introduction 93
9.2 Syllogism 94
9.3 The conditional predication principle 95
9.4 The conditional holistic principle 96
9.5 Discussions 98
9.6 Glossary 99

CHAPTER 10: JAINISM AND MODERN SCIENCE **101-110**
10.1 Analogies 101
10.2 Modern particle physics 103
10.3 Four forces in nature 105
10.4 Some further analogies 108
10.5 Concluding remarks 110

Epilogue **111-114**
1. Karmons and the karmic personal computer 111
2. Karmic fusion and vegetarianism 112
3. Karmons and obscuration of knowledge 112
4. The purification path 113
5. Self-restraint and the environmental issues 113

Appendices

APPENDIX 1: THE LIFE OF MAHAVIRA **117-120**
- A.1.1 Pursuit of the goal and enlightenment 118
- A.1.2 Career as a Tirthankara 119

APPENDIX 2: JAIN SCRIPTURES **121-124**
- A.2.1 Main scriptures 121
- A.2.2 Secondary scriptures 123

APPENDIX 3: CITATIONS **125-126**
- A. Axioms 125
- B. Texts 126

APPENDIX 4: PURIFICATION STAGES AND A GAME OF SNAKES AND LADDERS **127-128**

Bibliography **129-132**
- A. Texts and translations 129
- B. Modern works 130

ndex to Glossary **133-136**

General Index **137-142**

1
JAINS

1.1 INTRODUCTION

"Namo Arihantanam"

THIS IS THE FIRST line of the fundamental prayer of Jains which says "I pay my profound respect to any living person who has conquered his/her inner enemies (or his/her own lower nature)." This is irrespective of the religion, caste or social status of the individual.

Jainism is derived from the word *Jina* in the old Indian language of Ardha-Magadhi which was the common language in some parts of India 2,500 years or so ago—the word Jin means "the person who is a spiritual victor" and Jainism is now taken to mean the religion followed by Jains. However, to emphasise the path followed towards self-conquest rather than the religion, we will understand Jainism as *Jainness.* Indeed, the greeting used by Jains is *Jai Jinendra* which means "honour to the supreme *Jina*".

Loosely speaking, Jainism was founded by what are called Tirthankaras. Tirthankaras are the people who show the true way across the troubled ocean of life; they are leaders on a spiritual path. In all there were 24 Tirthankaras. The first of them was Rsabha.

Rsabha flourished ages ago according to Jain tradition, but the historicity of the religion has been unanimously accepted from the time of its 23rd Tirthankara, Parsva, about 2,800 years ago, (traditionally dated 872 B.C.-772 B.C.). The Jain logic and philosophy came into prominence at the time of its 24th Tirthankara, Mahavira, who was born in 559 B.C. and whose nirvana took place in 527 B.C. He was a contemporary of Gautama Buddha (563 B.C.-483 B.C.), the overlap being 36 years *but* they did not meet. It is commonplace to be confused

Fig. 1.1 Mahavira, the 24th Tirthankara. (Svetambara image; the eyes, lips and torso are marked.) His idol is distinguished by the emblem of a lion (from Sirohi, Rajasthan).

between these two leaders and even their religions. In iconography a simple distinction may be made by clothes—Mahavira is normally without these unlike Buddha (see, Fig. 1.1). Note that Buddha was in the process of enlightenment

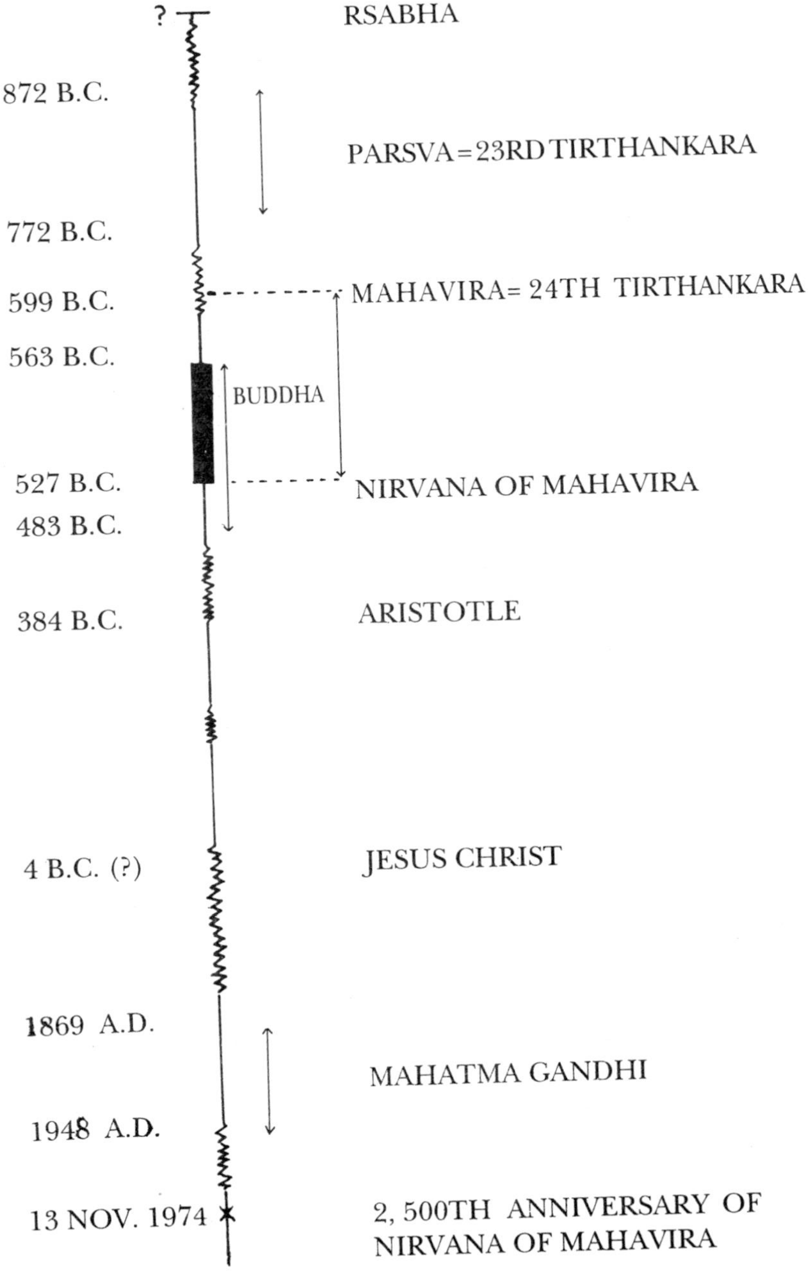

Fig. 1.2 Some important dates in Jain history, together with some other dates (Not to linear scale).

when Mahavira was at the peak of his career. For further details on Mahavira's life see Appendix 1. To bring these dates into perspective we may note that Aristotle was born in 384 B.C. and Jesus Christ around 4 B.C. It may be noted that India celebrated the 2,500th anniversary of Mahavira's nirvana between 13th November 1974 and 4th November 1975. These important dates are summarised in Fig. 1.2. One of the great admirers of the Jain religion was Mahatma Gandhi who was greatly influenced by certain Jains, e.g. Raychand/Srimad Rajchandra (see, Hay, 1970).

1.2 SOME CHARACTERISTICS OF JAINISM

The most important principle of Jainism is that of non-violence in thought and deed towards, not only fellow human beings, but even the smallest forms of life. Thus, most followers are vegetarians, avoiding even honey and alcohol which are believed to contain microscopic life.

Truthfulness, refraining from stealing and moderation in acquiring personal possessions and in sexual passions are other important facets. Meditation and general self-control also form a part of Jainism.

Jains do not believe in any external God who created and sustains the world, neither do they believe in any means of redemption outside themselves. The individual has to achieve his own salvation by right faith, right knowledge and right conduct. Salvation is believed to terminate the cycle of births and deaths and reincarnation, when the soul is finally liberated to eternal bliss and infinite knowledge.

Amongst themselves, there is no single leader such as a "Pope", neither has any person supreme authority. However, there are monks and certain teachers and lay leaders who are given particular respect. There are many scriptures (see Appendix 2) but no single book like the Bible. However, Umasvati's *Tattvartha-sutra* (second century A.D.) is the most comprehensive single treatise on Jainism. Notwithstanding these aids, however, the individual must ultimately find the truth for himself as no priest or scripture is believed to have all the answers. The principles are intended to be self-verifying so

Fig. 1.3 Parsva, the 23rd Tirthankara (Digambara image; the eyes, lips and torso are not marked). His idol is distinguished by the emblem of a snake (from Leeds, UK).

that the follower discovers truths for himself rather like a research worker in a laboratory.

Amongst the Jains, there are a few different schools. The main schools are "Digambara" and "Svetambara", both believe in idol-worship. However, their idols differ; in Svetambara eyes, lips and torso are marked, see Fig. 1.1 of Mahavira (Svetambara image) and Fig. 1.3 of the 23rd Tirthankara Parsva (Digambara image). The Digambara believe that their monks should renounce everything, even their clothes, whereas Svetambara monks wear white clothes. For the Digambara, the *Jina* can manifest no worldly activity and no longer has any bodily functions. There have been various reform movements. Two sub-groups of Svetambara, called Sthanakavasi and Terapantha, do not believe, in particular, in temples, including idol-worship. In addition, a sub-group of Digambara, called Taranapantha, also banned idol-worship. Table 1.1 gives an overview of different Jain schools with the originator, approximate time and some external signs of difference. Despite their different emphases, the basic beliefs of Jainism including belief in the 24 Tirthankaras are followed by all Jains.

Table 1.1 *Different schools of Jains with their originator, timing and some differences*

	Schools	Originator	Time	Comments
(1)	Digambara	Bhadrabahu	300 B.C.	Monks renounced clothes, temple-believers, no moksa for women.
Reform movements	Taranapantha	Taranswami	18th century	No temples, Prayer-halls
	Others	Banarsi Das (Todar Mal)	16th century 18th century	Full restraints, no rituals in temples.
(2)	Svetambara	Sthulabhadra?	300 B.C.	White-cotton clad monks, temple-believers, women can attain moksa.
Reform movements	Sthanakvasi	Lonka-Saha	15th century	No temples, monks wear a mouth-mask.
	Terapantha	Bhikanji	18th century	No temples and non-assistance except to monks.

1.3 AXIOMATIC APPROACH

Every spiritual path starts from some form of conviction or belief; it is argued in this book that the convictions of the Jains may be described by four basic axioms from which the whole path can be understood. These try to answer questions such as "Why are we imperfect?" and "What should we do about it?" If we were all immortal, perfect and eternally happy with fulfilment of every desire, there would be no place for any form of spiritual path. However, in reality, one goes through various ups and downs of life with pleasure and pain as the main themes of existence.

Further, one comes across all types of living entities who react differently to these various pressures. Why are there these differences? Why is one born handicapped? Why are there good people and bad? Is there anyone who could be "perfect"? Are death, decay and disease inevitable? Why are there different forms of life?

The four axioms constructed here attempt to answer these questions from the Jain standpoint and they are as follows:

Axiom 1: *"The soul exists in contamination with karmic matter and it longs to be purified."*

Axiom 2: *"Living beings differ due to the varying density and types of karmic matter."*

Axiom 3: *"The karmic bondage leads the soul through the states of existences (cycles)."*

Axiom 4A: *"Karmic fusion is due to perverted views, non-restraint, carelessness, passions and activities."*

Axiom 4B: *"Violence to oneself and others results in the formation of the heaviest new karmic matter, whereas helping others towards moksa with positive non-violence results into the lightest new karmic matter."*

Axiom 4C: *"Austerity forms the karmic shield against new karmons as well as setting the decaying process in the old karmic matter."*

These axioms look directly at the roots of the tree rather than its branches. The meaning and plausibility of these axioms is discussed in relation to the scriptures in the following chapters. Axioms 1-3 postulate Jain's scientific theory of karmons whereas Axioms 4A, 4B, 4C postulate its applications.

1.4 GLOSSARY

1. Tirthankara = Tīrthaṅkara
   Rsabha = Ṛṣabha
   Parsva = Pārśva
   Mahavira = Mahāvīra
   (Umasvati = Umāsvāti
   Tattvartha-sutra = Tattvārtha-sūtra)

2. *Jain Schools*
   Digambara = Digambara
   Svetambara = Śvetāmbara
   Sthanakavasi = Sthānakavāsī
   Taranapantha = Tāraṇapantha
   Terapantha = Terāpantha
   (Mouth mask = Muh-paṭṭi)

2
THEORY OF SOUL AND KARMIC MATTER (AXIOM 1)

Axiom 1: *"The soul exists in contamination with karmic matter and it longs to be purified."*

2.1 AXIOM

ABSTRACTLY, the concept of contaminated soul here implies that in the inhabited universe, it is composed of two distinct parts:

(a) non-living material;

(b) remainder; i.e. 'living' part.

The living part can be described as the 'pure soul' whereas the non-living material (non-pure part) is the karmic matter. (As an analogy, consider gold ore: the dross is 'karmic matter' and the left over 24-carat gold is the 'pure soul'.) Here karmic matter is actual physical material which makes the soul impure; it has nothing to do with the usual word 'karma', i.e. action. In the simplest terms, the pure soul contains all the important positive aspects of the living being and contamination by karmic matter produces the negative effects. However, this contamination by karmic matter is not natural for the soul which has an in-built longing to become separated from the matter.

In practice, this abstract idea implies that the aim is to acquire 'purity' of the soul or the 'victory' over the karmic matter. Karmic matter is regarded as the cause of all misery, etc. (Note that we are using the word 'soul' ambiguously as either 'pure soul' or 'contaminated soul', but the meaning should be obvious from the context.) To understand these concepts and the interaction of soul and karmic matter, we have to first understand Jain Theoretical Science. Jain Applied Science will be dealt with in Axiom 4.

2.2 THE BASIC CONCEPTS

2.2.1 *Soul*

It is believed that in nature there exists a non-material substance which has the following four main properties:[1]

1. Knowledge,
2. Perception (conation),
3. Bliss, and
4. Energy.

We will call these the four soul elements. The first two elements are cognitive functions of the soul and represent 'consciousness'. Bliss is a state which includes 'compassion' and 'total self-sufficiency'. Energy is an abstract force which powers the operation of the knowing and perceiving qualities of the soul. (Note that one of the words used in Jainism for soul is 'Jiva', i.e. living part.)

2.2.2 *Karmons and Karmic Matter*

Karmic matter consists of sub-atomic karmic particles which will be called *karmons* by us. These karmons float freely and randomly in space but they do not interact between each other. (Presumably the gravitational force is very small.) Among all sub-atomic particles, karmons are unique in the sense that they can only be absorbed by the soul, and cannot fuse by themselves, i.e. karmic matter as "molecules/aggregates" of karmons exist only in conjunction with the soul. Thus karmic matter increases by absorbing new karmons and decreases by dropping some karmons in space.

2.2.3 *Interaction*

In its purest state, the soul has infinite knowledge, perception, bliss and energy. The soul is sentient energy but in general, as this axiom states, the embodied soul is polluted by the karmic matter. The interaction of two highly contradictory elements, soul and karmic matter, could lead to severe distortion.

In particular, the karmic matter

(i) *obscures* the knowledge element of the soul,
(ii) *obscures* the perception element of the soul,
(iii) *defiles* the bliss element of the soul, and
(iv) *obstructs* the energy element of the soul.

Thus, due to karmic matter, one does not get the full advantage of the soul's pure qualities.

Note that bliss is the only element of the soul which gets transformed into something else; this transformation is analogous to changes in oneself under the influence of intoxication. This defilement in turn perverts the energy element. However, karmic matter can only survive in the soul, but the soul is self-supporting and has an inherent tendency to be free from karmic matter including the embodiment. This inherent tendency of the soul will be called the *freedom longing catalyst.*

2.3 TERMINOLOGY

2.3.1 *Karmic Process*

We now describe some important technical terms. The bond between soul and karmic matter is called *karmic bondage.* Note that the karmic matter is in association with the soul, but it has no direct contact with the soul.[2] However the karmic matter, coupled with the soul's perverted energy element, gives rise to a *karmic force-field/karmic field.* In turn, the force-field gives rise to *karmic influx,* the flow of karmons from all directions into the soul. Further, the karmic force coupled with the soul's obstructed energy element fuse the incoming karmons: we will call this process *karmic fusion.* The total karmic matter fused to the soul is thereby revised, and this dynamic karmic process continues. This process is depicted in Figs. 2.1-2.4. We will illustrate the soul containing karmic matter as a square with the karmic matter as the diagonal lines on it, and the karmic force-field as external parallel-lines (see, Fig. 2.1). In effect, Fig. 2.1 represents karmic-bondage and this representation will be used throughout the book. Fig. 2.2 shows a karmon (represented by a grey circle) attracted by the karmic field; the attraction is indicated by the force-lines being curved. The process of karmic fusion is indicated by the zig-zagged external boundary of the soul (Fig. 2.3). The increase in karmic matter and consequently stronger karmic force-field are indicated by more, and thicker, diagonal lines (Fig. 2.4).

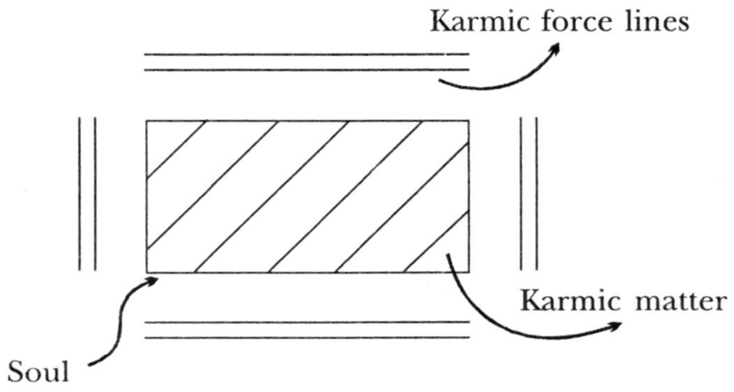

Fig. 2.1 The representation of a soul (= square) with karmic matter (= diagonal lines) and karmic force-lines (= parallel lines), i.e. karmic bondage.

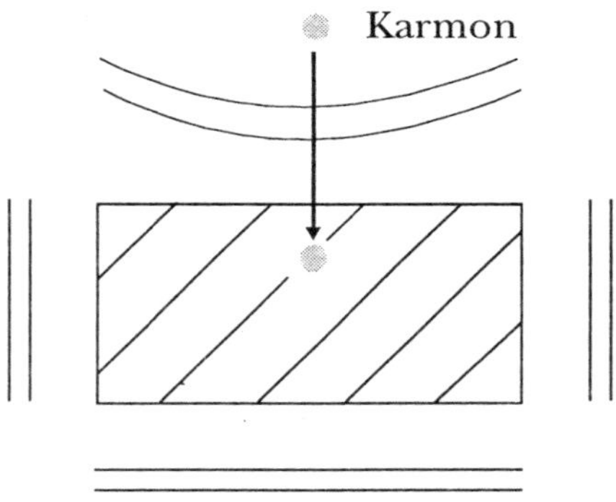

Fig. 2.2 An incoming karmon (= grey circle) and the karmic influx (= the curved lines).

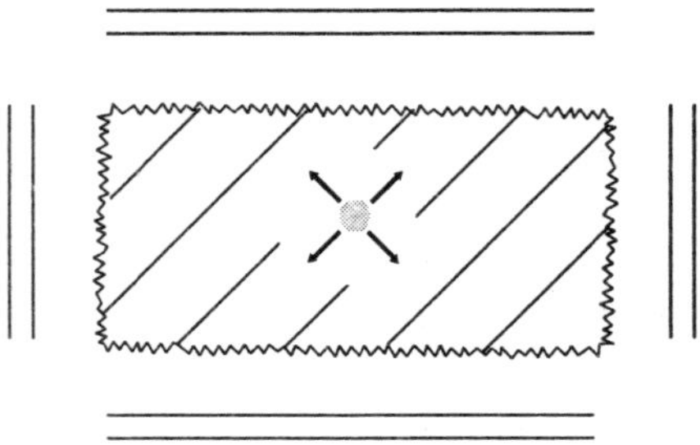

Fig. 2.3 Karmic fusion (zig-zagged boundary) with an incoming karmon of Fig. 2.2.

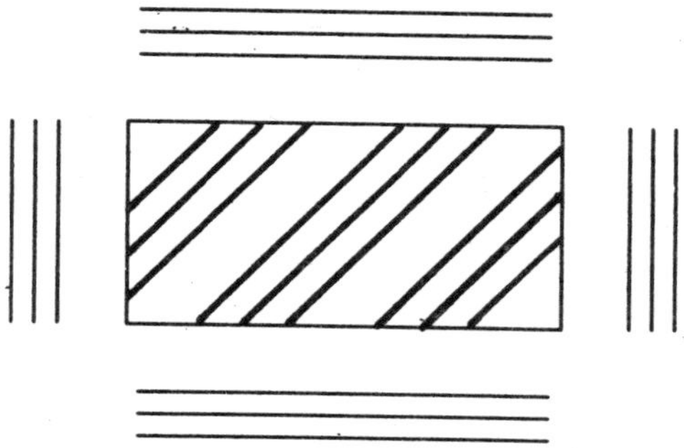

Fig. 2.4 Revised karmic matter (more and thicker diagonal lines, and more external lines) after fusion in Fig. 2.3.

It is important to distinguish between different states of the soul and the material forces in consequence of these states. Thus, the actual physical condition which allows the bombardment of the soul by karmons is karmic bondage, whereas the actual assimilation of karmons with the karmic matter is karmic fusion.

We have described karmic fusion but in the same way there is also *karmic decay/karmic fission* when karmons drop out/are emitted. However, if there is no karmic matter, the karmons cannot have any effect.

2.3.2 *Karmic Density*

Karmons exist in an undifferentiated form in nature, but the karmic force coupled with the obstructed soul energy introduces specific functions to the karmons so that they are differentiated.[3] It is assumed that the karmons recompose into 'heavy or light karmic matter', i.e. karmic matter with high or low density. *Heavy karmic matter* implies that the karmic bondage is strong, whereas *light karmic matter* implies that the karmic bondage is weak and it is therefore easier to remove this karmic matter from the soul. Thus there is a dynamic process of updating the karmic matter and therefore its functions. This process is depicted in Fig. 2.5, where the constituents of the light karmic matter are represented by open circles and those of the heavy karmic matter by dark circles rather than diagonal lines. This alternative representation highlights the constituents of the karmic matter.

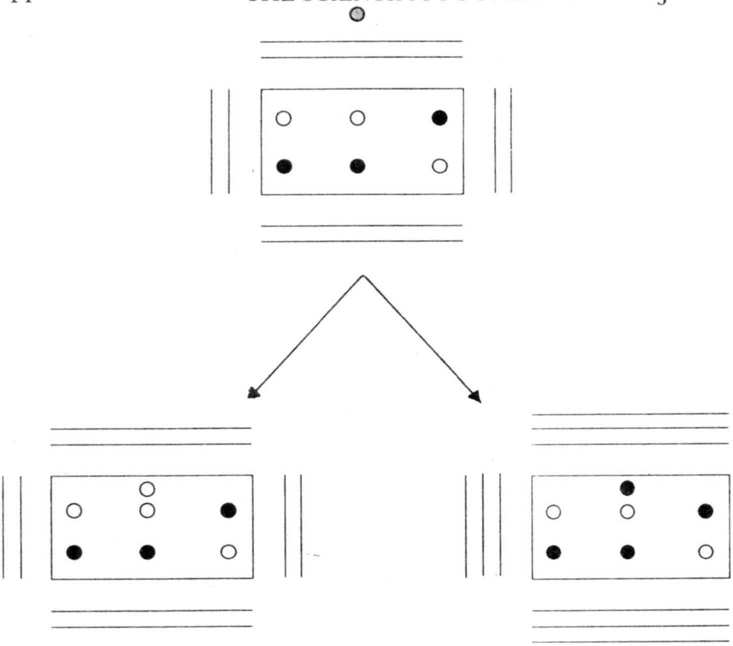

Fig. 2.5 The process of interactive activity between soul and a new incoming karmic particle (◎) in terms of light (○) and heavy karmic matter (●).

The karmic density distinguished above as light or heavy karmic matter, depends on the following factors:

(i) the number of karmons in karmic fusion,
(ii) different types of karmic matter/karmic components;
(iii) the potential energy in karmic decay; and
(iv) the time to decay of fused karmons.

The karmic components are the antithesis to the four basic soul elements and thus defile the bliss element, obscure the knowledge/perception element or obstruct the energy element of the soul. Further discussion is given in Ch. 3.

The factors (i)-(iv) given above also represent the order in which the karmic fusion takes place.

2.3.3 *Long-term Equilibrium State*

We have described above the short-term state of the soul. We now describe the long-term equilibrium state of the soul. When all the karmic matter is removed from the soul through the emission of karmons, what is left is the pure soul, that is, it has infinite levels of the four elements of the soul described above in Sec. 2.2.2. There are two stages in the attainment of this state. Firstly, karmic influx is stopped by creating a *karmic force shield* which implies the total end of the inflow of new karmons. The next stage is the total dropping of the accumulated karmic matter, i.e. *total karmic decay/fission.* When all the karmons have been emitted, the soul no longer has a karmic field and thus has attained its full potential: this is the *liberated state.* Thus there is everlasting karmic fusion and fission except under the liberated state. (How these are achieved in practice will be left to Chs. 5-7.) Fig. 2.6 illustrates this mechanism with a representation similar to that of Fig. 2.5. Fig. 2.6a is the soul with karmic matter, and Fig. 2.6b shows influence of incoming karmons on the karmic force. Fig. 2.6c shows the karmic force shield to cease the karmic influx and Fig. 2.6d indicates karmic decay of the last karmon under the karmic force shield. Fig. 2.6e shows the liberated soul, with the release of infinite energy etc. indicated by the emanating rays.

The idea of karmons is profound. One can compare the concept with that of psychological responses under different circumstances, but these responses, of course, do not explain the psychology of other living beings nor the inner mechanism.

2.3.4 *The Nine Reals*

We have described the concept of non-sentience which includes:

(1) karmic matter,
(2) karmic bondage/fusion,
(3) karmic force/influx,
(4) karmic force-shield,
(5) karmic decay/fission, and
(6) liberation.

With (7) soul,
(8) heavy karmic matter, and
(9) light karmic matter included.

we have what are called the nine fundamental reals (facts) of Jain Science [Note that category (1) is very large and includes six existents to be described later] for the standard order of these reals, see § 2.5.

It is claimed that these reals have existed eternally and form the essential part of the natural laws: they explain the evolution of the universe. To quote (from *Mahapurana*):

"Know that the world is uncreated, as time itself is;

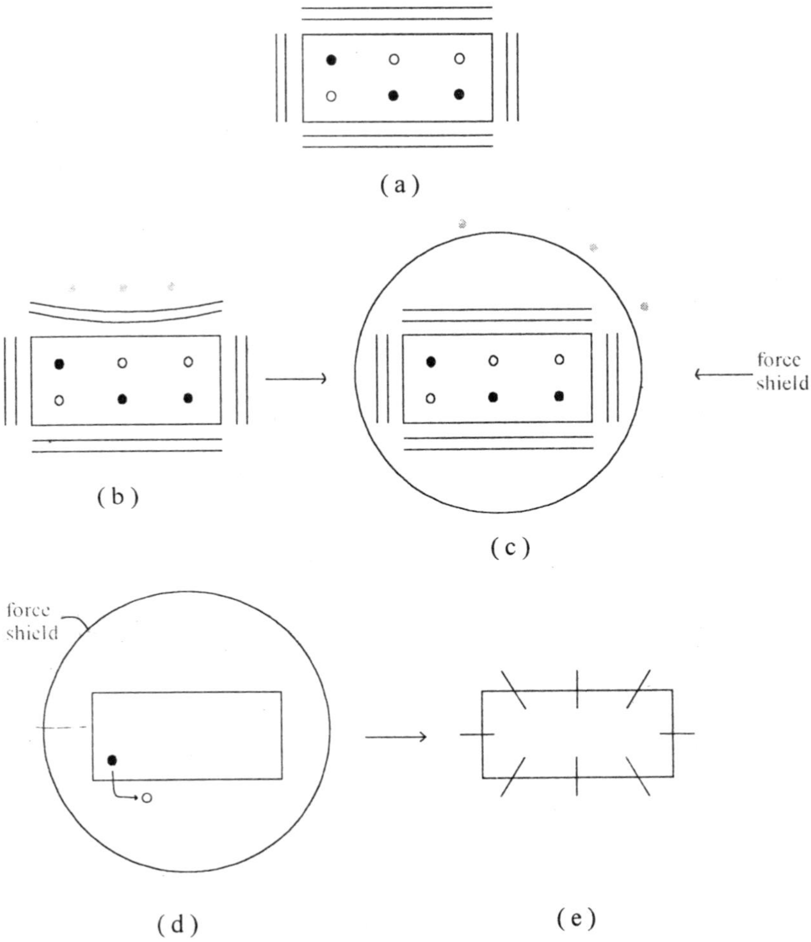

Fig. 2.6 The definitions of some reals: (a) karmic bondage; (b) karmic influx and force; (c) karmic force shield; (d) karmic decay under shield; and (e) liberated soul.

without beginning and end,
and is based on the principles, life and the rest."

The 'principles' here mean the nine reals—'life' means the soul and the 'rest' implies the other eight reals. Therefore, no particular being is the creator of the universe. Belief is in the reals of Jain Science, consequently it is sometimes called a trans-atheistic religion rather than an atheistic religion. One of the reasons put forward against the existence of a personal god, as a creator is as follows. If the world was created by someone, then this would imply that the alleged creator had a desire to create as are beings of a low level of life in their spiritual evolution, i.e. far from being a perfect-soul. Further, by definition, a higher being would only create a perfect world, not an unequal/unbalanced world. Thus, a higher being could not be the creator.

2.4 IMPORTANT ANALOGIES

We have defined the various terms above by using only the concepts of physics, but otherwise not introducing any analogies, which have tended to make the literature seem obscure. However, karmons, soul, etc. can only be known through their properties as such. Since these can be comprehended only through their effects, we will therefore give various analogies which have been used to give ideas of their different properties. Nevertheless, it should be borne in mind that, for instance, *light can exhibit both the properties of particles and waves depending on the way in which it is considered, but light is light.* The properties of a substance cannot uniquely

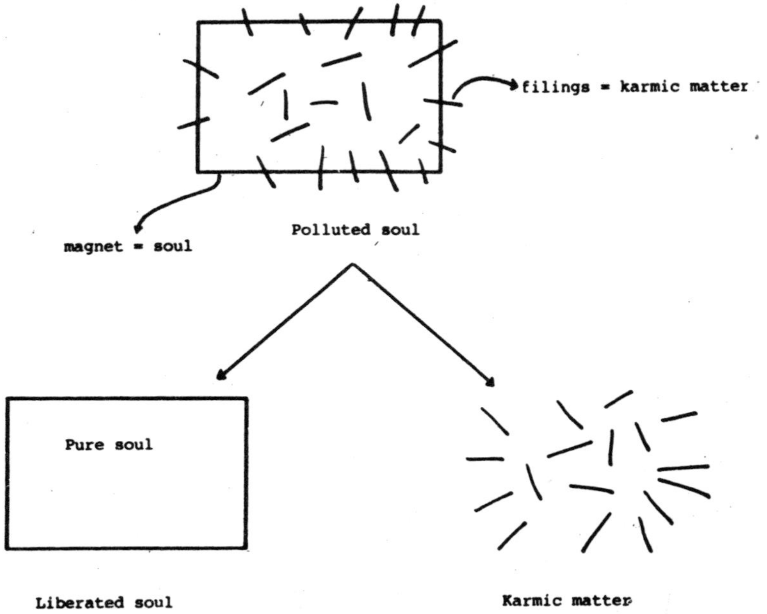

Fig. 2.7 The soul as a magnet, and karmic matter as filings.

determine the substance itself. This rationale very much applies to karmons and the soul.

2.4.1 *Magnetism*

We may regard the polluted soul as a magnet. It attracts iron-filings which can be considered as karmons. The magnetic force lines are equivalent to karmic force lines, the joining of the iron filings to a magnet can be looked at as karmic fusion, that is, they get strongly bonded to the soul. Creating a force field shield which stops new filings from being attracted is a form of insulation. The shedding of old particles in the force field, of course, implies demagnetisation so there is no attraction and when all the particles are dropped, the soul is free from the magnetic element of this karmic matter and what is left is the liberated soul. This is shown in Fig. 2.7. As mentioned before, it should be remembered that this is only an analogy since karmic matter attracts its own particles (karmons) unlike filings which do not attract each other.

2.4.2 *Miscellaneous Analogies*

Another analogy is with petrol. This is a refined stage of crude oil, thus in nature the energy is obscured because of the impurity and only refinement leads to the full combustive power of petrol. Obviously, the refined stage is the pure soul and impurities are karmic matter.

Another comparison which is made is that the impure soul is like an oiled cloth. This cloth can attract, because of the moisture, dust particles which are karmic particles, where the bond between the cloth and the oil is like karmic bondage. Note that the nature of the soul remains invariant under adaptation to a particular body's dimensions, like a cloth which can be folded into various shapes without any alteration in its mass. Finally, an interesting analogy is how a virus can effect the body resulting in changes (e.g. long illness); in the same way, karmic matter can influence the soul.

2.5 GLOSSARY

1. *Nine Reals (Tattva)*
   Soul = Jiva
   Karmic matter = (part of 'Ajiva' = 'insentient')

Karmic force/influx = Āsrava
Karmic bondage/fusion = Bandha
Karmic force shield = Saṃvara
Karmic fission/decay = Nirjarā
Liberation = Mokṣa
Heavy karmic matter = Pāpa
Light karmic matter = Puṇya

2. *Soul's Elements (Guṇa)*
Bliss = Sukha
Knowledge = Jñāna
Perception = Darśana
Energy = Vīrya
Freedom longing (catalyst) = Bhavyatva
(Liberated soul = Siddha,
Perfect being = Arihanta).

3. *Karmic Dynamics and Karmic Density*
Number of karmons in karmic fusion = Pradeśa
Potential energy in karmon-decay = Anubhava
Time to decay of fused karmons = Sthiti
Different type of karmic matter (karmic components) = Prakṛti
Emission = Udaya
Suppression = Upaśama

NOTES

1. P.S. Jaini, p. 114. "Jainas speak of the 'innumerable qualities' of the soul. Nevertheless, it can legitimately be said that the presence of those qualities which have been briefly discussed above—perception, knowledge, bliss, and energy—are sufficient to define the soul as a totally distinct and unique entity, an existent separate from all others."
2. P.S. Jaini, p. 113. "It should be made clear that Jainas view the soul's involvement with karma as merely an "association" (*ekakṣetrāvagāha,* literally, occupying the same locus); there is said to be no actual *contact* between them..."
3. P.S. Jaini, p. 112. "Karmic matter is said to be found 'floating free' in every part of occupied space. At this stage it is undifferentiated; various types (prakṛti) of karma, classifiable by function, are molded from these simpler forms only after interaction with a given soul has begun."

3
HIERARCHY OF LIFE (AXIOM 2)

Axiom 2: *"Living beings differ due to the varying density and types of karmic matter."*

3.1 THE AXIOM

How does the karmic matter divide different living species? If we accept Axiom 2, then it says that the differing density of the karmic matter is one of the main reasons for the differences between living species, i.e. the purer the basic elements of the soul, the higher is the form of life. We will define fully types of karmic matter (heavy, light) in the next chapter i.e., the components into which karmic matter gets differentiated.

3.2 LIFE-UNITS AND LIFE-AXIS

The degree of soul-purity can be quantified in a relative way. We may define for convenience a unit of soul-purity as being that degree of purity of the soul which leads to 100 life-units in the average human being. This figure of 100 might be compared to the intelligence quotient for our ease of understanding. Thus at one extreme, the pure soul will have an infinity of life-units whereas an insentient object will have zero life units. Thus we can represent the soul's purity or the life-units of the living beings along a line taking value from zero to infinity: we will call this the life-axis. Note that as the degree of soul-purity varies from zero to infinity the density of the karmic matter will vary from infinity to zero, inversely as it were.

The two main components of the soul's purity can be regarded as the number of senses related to energy/bliss elements, and the level of intelligence related to knowledge/perception elements described in Ch. 2. Bearing these in mind, we will further divide the life-axis in the next section. These divisions have always existed qualitatively in Jain Science, but we can now quantify them.

3.3 DIVISION OF THE LIFE AXIS ACCORDING TO THE NUMBER OF SENSES/INTELLIGENCE

The lowest forms of life are the micro-organisms which possess only one sense, that of touch. These are infinitesimal and can only exist as part of a larger body (living or non-living) and therefore they should have very few life-units, say 10^{-4} life-units.

The next stage of life is another group of one-sensed micro-organisms which take the subtlest possible unit of matter as their homes and these beings are earth-bodied, water-bodied, air-bodied and fire-bodied.[1] We will denote earth, water, air or

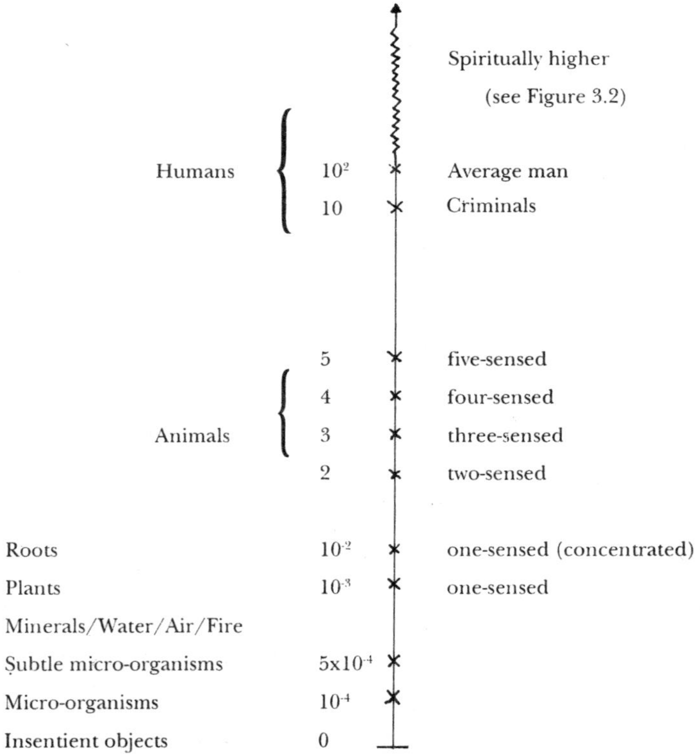

Fig. 3.1 The life-axis giving the degree of the soul's purity for different beings (Not to linear scale).

fire bodied beings in Fig. 3.1 by a life-unit of 5×10^{-4}. Next are plants which are rated higher than the preceding, having gross individual bodies, and we will rate them at 10^{-3} life-units. It is interesting to note that one can distinguish between the various concentrations of life in plants. These are shown in Fig. 3.1. For example, onions are believed to have a more concentrated form of life than apples since one seed of an apple gives rise to thousands of apples, so the life gets subdivided whereas an onion root gives only one onion in the process and, therefore, we can regard the life in an onion not 10^{-3} life-units but something like 10^{-2} life-units. This comment also applies to trees. Further, plants or dead flesh infested by innumerable micro-organisms will also have a higher degree of life-units.

When some of the karmic matter is removed, then the next higher form of life appears in which the being has two senses, a body and a mouth/tongue. The two senses are touch and taste as it appears say, for example, in seashells, mussels, etc. We give these 2 life-units.

The next stage of higher life has, of course, three senses, where it has also a nose; that is, having the additional sense of smell, for example, an insect without eyes. We regard these as having 3 life-units. Further reduction of karmic matter leads to four-sensed beings which develop eyes or the sense of sight, for example, bees, flies, etc. These are assigned 4 life-units. Finally, we have beings with ears or a sense of hearing, for example, horses, camels, etc. These have five senses—touch, taste, smell, sight and hearing, i.e. they have a body, mouth, nose, eyes and ears. These are called five-sensed beings. Among the five-sensed beings is the first level of animal life where there is no sense of time, viz., what is past, what is present and what is future. These are given 5 life-units on the life-axis. After animal life, the next stage is the human body which has a sense of time or a high degree of coherence in addition to the five senses above. This class is very broad, and thus, for example, a criminal would receive a lower score along the life-axis than a humanitarian. For an average human, the base score of 100 life-units has been agreed so that a criminal may score only 10 life-units. This completes a

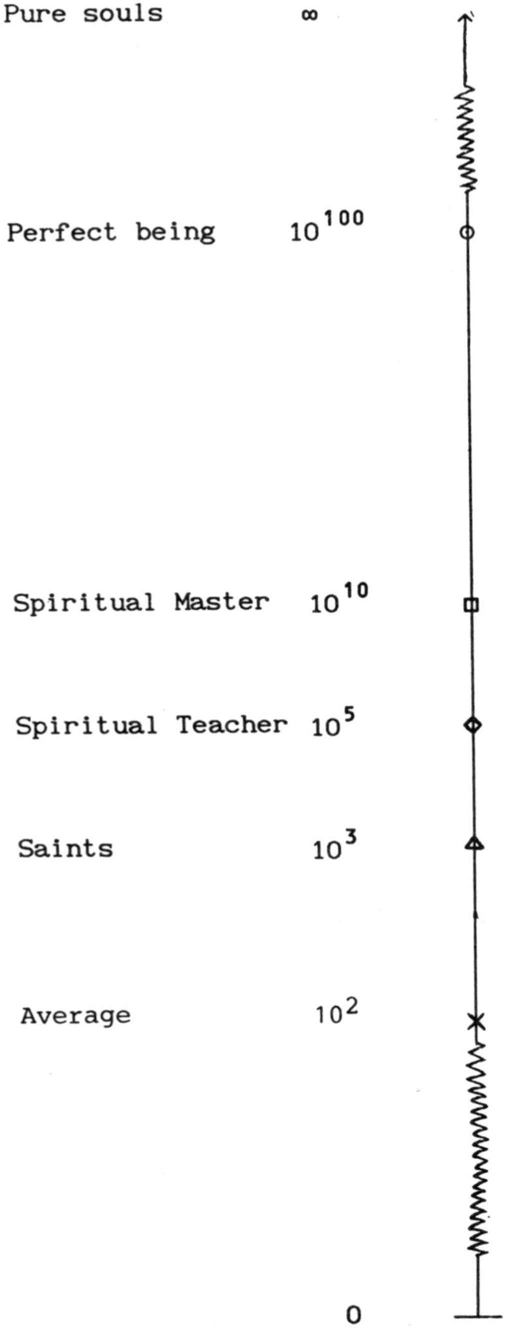

Fig. 3.2 Five spiritually higher beings on the life-axis (Not to linear scale).

description of the life-units along the life-axis in Fig. 3.1.

Some form of ascending scores can be connected to the idea of the spiritual advancement of individuals. These are shown in Fig. 3.2. At the first stage are the saints who are supposed to walk on the spiritual path with single-mindedness. Those at the second stage are those spiritual teachers who have experienced the truth. The third are the spiritual masters who practice what they preach, being the true masters. The fourth category are the perfect living beings who have conquered their inner enemies. The nominal life-units for these categories are 10^3, 10^5, 10^{10}, 10^{100}, respectively. Those in the final category are pure souls (liberated souls) which are a form of absolute energy. The score for the liberated soul is at the point of infinity, as it has no impurity (not even a body). (Most Jains today might not accept these statements literally although some early followers believed that teachers of other religions could reach the higher states.)

3.4 THE FOUR STATES OF EXISTENCE

Every living being possesses varying degrees of sensitivity due to its mental state. We describe the four main directions, which the mental state can take. The state with the highest agonising point is the hellish state. The extreme state of pleasure is called the heavenly state. This is a hedonistic pleasure but does not correspond to the state of bliss. The state where the living being does not know what is tomorrow or did not know what was yesterday, is the animalistic state. The state of the equilibrium point between the pleasure and the pain is the average human state.

Every living being is capable of taking the above four directions of these mental states, namely:

Hellish state, Heavenly state, Human state, and Animalistic state and are represented symbolically in Fig. 3.3 in the form of a swastika; the central point being the mind. (Note that the Nazis misused the symbol by using its reflection.) These directions are again influenced by the density of the karmic matter, and they should be taken into account while placing a living being on the life-axis of a given species.

The literal interpretations of these states correspond to the

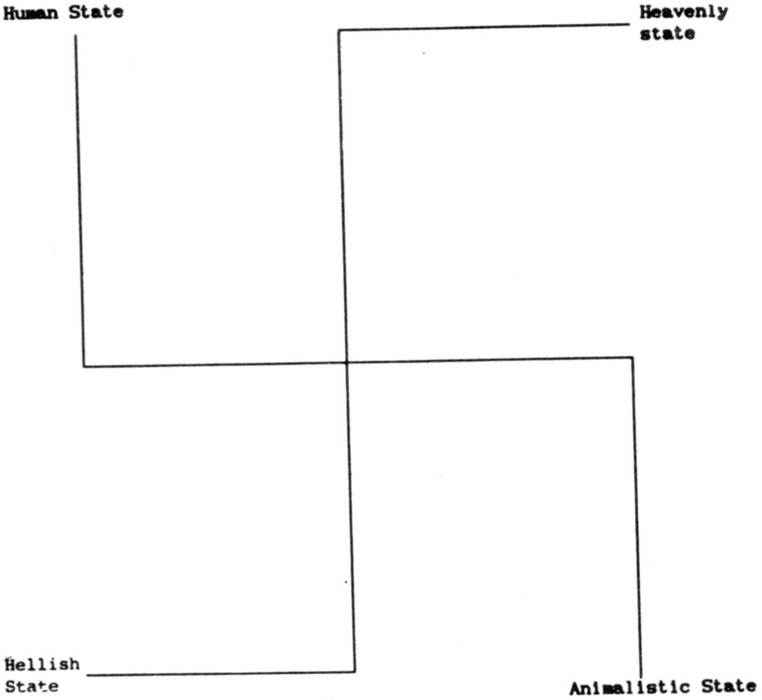

Fig. 3.3 Four directions of the mental state in living beings.

four states of existence: hell-being, heavenly being, animal/plant life and human being respectively. At the central point passes the axis of rotation through different lives. Our approach follows Kundakunda whereby "the self by its own thought activity creates for itself the four forms of these beings" (see, Appendix, 3B, q.3.1).

3.5 GLOSSARY

Soul/living being = Jīva
Non-soul/Insentient object = Ajīva
Micro-organisms = Nigoda

Five-spiritually high (= Pañca-parameṣṭhin)
Saint = Sādhu
Spiritual teacher = Upādhayāya
Spiritual master = Ācārya
Perfect being = Arihaṇta
Pure soul/liberated soul = Siddha

Four Existences (= Gati)

Heavenly being = Deva

Hellish being = Nāraki

Animal/Plant life = Tiryañca

Human = Manuṣya

NOTES

1. P.S. Jaini, p. 109. "At the very bottom of this scale hence comprising the lowest form of life, are the so-called *nigoda*. These creatures are sub-microscopic and possess only one sense, that of touch. They are so tiny and undifferentiated that they lack even individual bodies;..... Just above the nigoda is another group of single-sense organisms whose members take the very elements—the subtlest possible units of matter—as their bodies; hence they are called the earth bodies (*pṛthvī-kāyika*), water-bodies (*āpo-kāyika*), fire bodies (*tejo-kāyika*), and air bodies (*vāyu-kāyika*), respectively."

4
CYCLES OF BIRTH AND DEATH (AXIOM 3)

Axiom 3: "*The karmic bondage leads the soul through the states of existences (cycles).*"

4.1 THE AXIOM

IN AXIOM 2 we concentrated only on the static situation of living beings through one life-span rather than the dynamic situation of various life cycles. The question arises as to whether there exists a cycle of birth and death. This axiom assumes that there is such a cycle. On death the soul is set free of physical body and is thus ready to move on under its own propulsion. From Axiom 2 it is quite clear that the amount of karmic matter will be responsible for the next placement on the life-axis. However, the following questions do arise:

(1) What is meaningfully transported from one life to the next?

(2) What form of science can allow such a transportation?

4.2 THE KARMIC COMPONENTS

To answer the above questions, we assume that the karmic matter gets differentiated into eight specific types by the activities of the contaminated soul. We call these types the karmic components.

We will view the karmic components as negative forces arising from the karmic matter and perverted energy element of the soul. Recall the four basic elements of the soul: bliss, energy, knowledge and perception and its intrinsic freedom-longing catalyst. Fig. 4.1 sketches the state of the soul at a fixed point in time. On the positive scale we have infinite bliss, energy, knowledge and perception. Underlying these elements is the strong freedom-longing catalyst. On the negative side corresponding to bliss, we have a component which defiles this element. This component will be called the Bliss-Defiling karmic component; we will write it as the "a-component". The a-component has an Insight-Defiling sub-component (a_1) and a Conduct-Defiling sub-component (a_2) which we will write as the a_1 sub-component and the a_2 sub-component respectively. Recall that the Defiling-Component changes the overall structure of the soul; that is, the process leads to a very fundamental transformation of its elements, e.g. change of personality under intoxication. Similarly, we have the second negative component which obstructs the operation of the energy element and which we will call the Energy-Obstructing Karmic Component (b) and denote by b-component. This makes the soul not only work with restricted energy but it becomes an accomplice in the process of karmic fusion with the existing karmic matter as well as in karmic decay. Similarly, we have the third and fourth karmic components, the Knowledge-Obscuring Component (c) and the Perception-Obscuring Component (d) which we will write as the c-component and the d-component respectively. Note again that these last two components only obscure the two soul elements and do not defile the soul.

These four components are operating at every instant and are described as "destructible" (decaying) components in a given life-cycle. We will call them the "Primary-Components".

The other four components are Secondary Components which refer to the next embodiment and indirectly they attack the freedom-longing catalyst. These components are named "Feeling-Producing" (e), "Body-Producing" (f), "Longevity-Determining" (g), and "Environmental-Determining" (h). We will write these as the e-component, f-component, g-compo-nent and h-component respectively. These four components react only slowly to the process of fusion and decay at a particular moment, except at the time just before the beginning of the next life-cycle. Table. 4.1 summarizes these components:

Table 4.1. *Eight karmic components*

Primary Components (Destructive in this cycle)	Secondary Components (Non-destructive in this cycle)
(a) Bliss-defiling	(e) Feeling producing
(a_1) Insight deluding	(e_1) Pleasure producing
(a_2) Conduct deluding	(e_2) Pain producing
(b) Energy obstructing	(f) Body producing
(c) Knowledge obscuring	(g) Longevity determining
(d) Perception obscuring	(h) Environmental determining

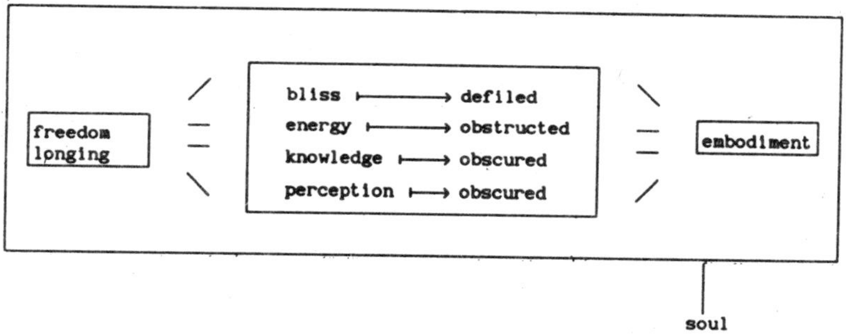

Fig. 4.1 State of a soul at a fixed point in time with its elements and the effect of karmic matter.

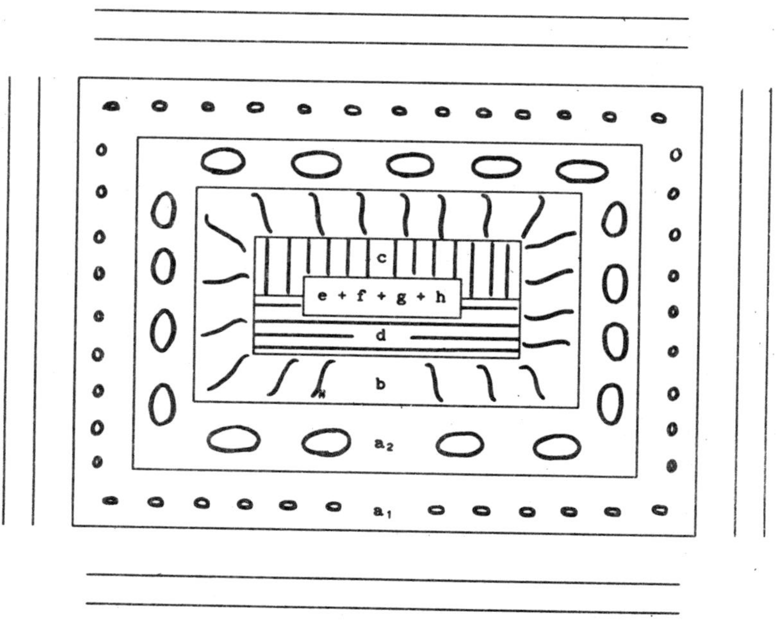

Fig. 4.2 Eight karmic components of karmic matter on a contaminated soul with the hierarchy of karmic components—the outer are more active than the inner.

Although all karmic components operate independently, the defiling component-a plays a central role since it defiles the soul and allows other components to operate. In fact, the component-b is influenced by the existence of this defiling process. Fig. 4.1 illustrates the static aspect of the interaction. Fig. 4.2 shows the hierarchic influence of these components on the soul, so that the karmic components in the outer rectangles are more active at every instant than those in the inner rectangles, e.g. the a_1-component and a_2-component are more active than the b-component and so on, whereas the components e, f, g and h operate slowly. (We can compare these karmic energy-levels to those of the electrons in the inner and outer shells of an atom.)

4.3 WHAT GETS TRANSPORTED?

As described above, the four secondary karmic components are responsible for various aspects of the next incarnation. In particular, the body-karmic component is said to generate two 'subtle bodies' underlying the manifest physical body: (1) the *luminous capsule*, which maintains the vital functions (temperature, etc.) of the organism; and (2) the *karmic body*, constituting the sum total of the karmic matter present in the soul at a given time. The existence of such kinds of bodies is important to the theory of rebirth since they constitute a vehicle whereby a soul moves under its own power from one incarnation to the next.[1]

At the moment of death, the Body-Producing karmic component (f-component) has pre-programmed, as it were,

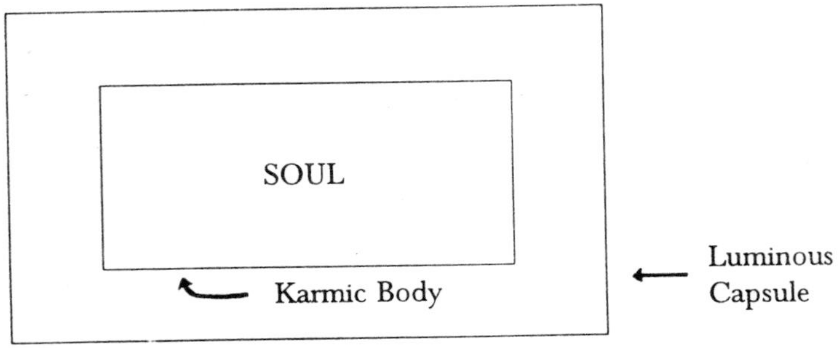

Fig. 4.3 A soul in transition: with its karmic body and luminous capsule.

the particular conditions of the coming embodiment. This information is carried in the karmic body. At death the soul is released from its physical body and is said to travel in a straight line almost instantaneously to the destination which its accompanying karmic matter has pre-determined.[2]

The transported material is very much like a hermetically sealed capsule (the luminous capsule) containing the karmic body and the soul (see, Fig. 4.3) stopping the flux and shedding of any karmons. In spite of the inherent propulsion due to the soul energy at the time of death it cannot travel too far before it enters a physical body in an egg or womb. The stationary medium as defined in § 4.4 ensures this unless it is being liberated.

4.4 SIX EXISTENTS

We now consider the Jain Laws on Nature which allow various operations such as the interaction between soul and karmons, next embodiment, liberation of the soul, etc. According to Jain Science, the universe is comprised of six "existents". These are:

(1) soul,
(2) matter,
(3) space,
(4) time,
(5) dynamic medium, and
(6) stationary medium.

In contrast with standard physics where one deals with matter in time and space coordinate systems, in Jain Science it is the soul which is to be studied in terms of time, space and matter. These all are regarded as 'substances' which is also a helpful way of considering them.

Space. Jain space is sub-divided into two types. The first, which is occupied by the other five existents, and the second which is empty. We shall call these simply *occupied and unoccupied space* respectively. "Occupied space" is equivalent to the manifest universe in which all the other five existents are confined. The inherent quality of occupied space is its ability to provide a "home" for the other five existents and it is divisible into infinitesimally small *space points,* which have dimension but cannot be further sub-divided.[3] The idea that the occupied universe is bounded is quite implicit in this formulation. Further, the boundary between occupied space and unoccupied space is quite important as we shall see later.

Dynamic and Stationary Media. 'The Dynamic Medium' allows interaction/motion to take place between/within soul and matter, whereas 'the Stationary Medium' allows equilibrium/stability between/within soul and matter. The usual analogy is that the dynamic medium is like water allowing the movement of a fish whereas the stationary medium is like the shade of a tree which allows travellers to rest. Thus soul/matter has the inherent quality to 'go' or 'stop', but these two media make these operations possible. In general, the 'Go-mode' includes developing, interacting, moving, etc. and the 'Stop-mode' is the opposite.

The two media are non-atomic, inactive, formless and continuous. These co-exist and we can regard dynamic and stationary media as secondary and tertiary space respectively. The logic behind these two media is elegantly summarized as follows by Basham (1958, p. 76), where we have substituted our terminology in this quotation:

"The existence of dynamic medium as a secondary space is proved to the Jain's satisfaction from the fact of motion; this must be caused by something; it cannot be due to time or the atoms, since they have no spatial extension, and that which is spaceless cannot give rise to movement in space; it cannot be due to the soul, since souls do not fill the whole universe, but motion is possible everywhere; it cannot be due to space, for space extends even beyond the universe, and if space was the basis of motion the bounds of the universe would fluctuate, which they do not; therefore motion must be caused by some other substance which does not extend beyond the universe, but pervades the whole of it; this is what is called dynamic medium. The existence of 'stationary medium' is proved by similar arguments."

The first four existents—soul, matter, space and time—do not themselves undergo any changes due to the two media, but they function in so far as soul and matter in either 'Go-mode' through space or 'Stop-mode' in space. Thus in particular, the dynamic medium allows karmic fusion/fission whereas the stationary medium allows the state of karmic bondage. Further, the dynamic medium will allow the soul to travel to the next embodiment whereas the stationary medium will allow it to be planted in a womb.

We have regarded the two existents as media for motion and rest but these can be viewed as two forces: *Dynamic* and *Stationary forces.* These operate on the non-living as well as the living. Their relation with four forces in Nature recognised by Modern Physics will be discussed in Ch. 10.

Time. Time is also not affected by the other existents. The Jains believe that time is digital, i.e. consists of an infinite series of discrete time points each dimensionless, for example, whenever a particular instant of time is recorded. Time as an existent has no beginning or end. Jains have regarded time as a fourth dimension in space and time interaction; for a detailed discussion involving time, space and other existents, see Basham (1958, p. 78).

Matter (Pudgala). It is important to realise that "pudgala" will be translated as "matter" but in Jain Science the word also includes "physical energy". The word is formed from the two words *pum* (joining) and *gala* (breaking). This gives central importance to the formation and destruction of matter; destruction has the implication of converting matter into energy and energy into matter. The modern word is "mass-energy" but the emphasis here is on matter-energy.

Matter is finally composed of what may be described as *the ultimate particle (U.P.).* These are the smallest indivisible particles which we write "U.P." They can be aggregated in many different ways so that they produce every form of organic and inorganic matter but exclude the soul.

The finest form of matter is called *fine-fine* and contains a finite number of U.P.'s. Thus, these are the particles from which the karmons are formed. The lowest number of karmons are in a *karmic body,* and a much higher number in a *karmic capsule.* One U.P. occupies at most one space-point. The physical energy in *fine-fine* is analogous to electricity. The next category of matter is *fine* which has several U.P.'s and thus is molecular. Like the *fine-fine, fine* is too small to be detected by these senses. Recall that molecules are aggregations of atoms in scientific terminology. Karmic matter on a contaminated soul is a *fine* matter which has an *infinite number of karmons.*

The karmic matter constituting the karmic body is extremely fine. Although slightly less so, the karmic capsule is also very fine and invisible and it is found in all polluted souls. These bodies are so subtle that they pass through and may be passed through by everything. (One is reminded of a neutrino's behaviour here.)

The luminous capsule is translated by some writers as magnetic body or electrical body. It is also claimed (C.R. Jain, 1929) that it is a body of luminous matter and is a necessary link between the other two bodies of the soul, the karmic body and the physical gross body. A link of this kind is needed because the matter of the karmic body is too fine and that of the physical body too gross to allow any direct or immediate interaction between them.

The next category is *fine-gross.* The things in this category can be recognised by the senses but are not so gross as to be visible; e.g. heat, sound, etc. which can be perceived by the four senses of touch, taste, smell or hearing, but are not tangible.

The fourth category is *gross-fine* which is grosser than *fine-gross* which cannot be seen. It is matter which looks gross or tangible but which cannot be grasped, e.g. light. Thus here light is regarded as an aggregation of particles. We can draw attention here to the notion that light is sometimes to be thought of as a stream of particles but at other times as an electro-magnetic wave (see, for example, Pedler, 1981). Recent discussions have led to a more convincing classification of light, electricity, sound, gas etc. with gross-fine and fine-gross with respect to the particle sizes rather than the visibility criterion (see, Jain N.L., 1993).

The fifth category is *gross* which is equivalent to liquids and the last category is *gross-gross* which is equivalent to solids. These are the different states of matter. A summary of this classification of matter is given in Table 4.2. We have given here one type of classification of the matter, but Jains also use an alternative classification of twentythree main types of 'groups' of matter, depending upon the degree of compactness of the U.P.'s in space (see, Zaveri, 1975; pp. 58-61).

Table 4.2 *Classification of matter*

Name	Definition	Examples
0 U.P.	Ultimate particle	
1 Fine-fine	"Atoms" formed from U.P.'s	Karmons, Range of karmic body to karmic capsule, Nuclear energy, Electricity
2 Fine	"Molecules/Aggregates" from karmons	Karmic matter
3 Fine-gross	Can be recognized by senses other than eye	Sound, Heat, Gases
4 Gross-fine	Can be perceived by eye but cannot be grasped	Light
5 Gross	Combines itself without external material	Liquid
6 Gross-gross	All the rest	Solid

As the soul has its characteristics of life including bliss, energy, knowledge and perception elements, matter has its characteristics of lifelessness, touch, flavour, smell and colour.

The important principle is that each quality produced by elementary particles undergoes constant changes of mode along its respective continuum. Thus, matter and energy may be regarded as one and the same thing, i.e. *sound, light, heat,* etc. are matter but their mode is energy. These Jain concepts of matter and energy do not seem to include all the concepts of Modern Physics but nevertheless, these are compatible (see, Ch. 10). On the other hand, Jain Science explains the phenomenon of Mind over Matter. It shows how finer karmic matter from karmons and the soul are interrelated.

The soul. Occupied space contains an infinite number of souls. Each soul has an uncountable number of space points but exists within the physical limits of its current corporeal shape. Liberated souls are all distinct and are not under constraints of time, dynamic or stationary forces and are on the highest point of the boundary between occupied space and unoccupied space. The highest point on the boundary is perhaps similar to a black hole in the sense that the standard laws of physics are not applicable in a black hole. When all karmic matter, even the finest (*fine-fine*) is removed, the soul will move to this highest point. The soul now attains infinite bliss, energy, knowledge and perception.

Note that in Jain, the mind is regarded as the sixth sense, made up of matter which acts as a processor of input from five senses and it should not be confused with consciousness—the knowledge and perception elements.

4.5 JAIN PARTICLE PHYSICS

Matter has one of five colours, one of five flavours, one of two odours and one each of the four pairs of touches. These are given below:

Five types of colour: Black, red, yellow, white, blue.

Five types of flavour: Sweet, bitter, pungent, acidic, astringent.

Two types of odour: Good smell, bad smell.

Eight types of touch in four pairs: Hot/cold, wet/dry, (smooth/rough), hard/soft, light/heavy.

The ultimate particle (U.P.) has the following properties:

One of the five colours,

One of the five flavours,

One of the two types of odour,

One of the four touches in pairs of either wetness/dryness or hot/cold.

Thus, it leads to 200 different "primary U.P.'s". It is shown that wetness and dryness possess varying intensities which are integers. These combine together to produce composite bodies. The fundamental condition is that the U.P.'s in combination must possess more than one unit intensity of dryness or wetness. These cannot combine if the intensity is only one unit. Also, if x and y are the intensities of wetness of two U.P.'s, then to combine them

$$|x-y| \leq 2, x=2,...; y=2,....$$

The same applies to two U.P.'s with different dryness. There are no restrictions on the composition of two U.P.'s, with one U.P. of x units of dryness and another of y units of wetness, except that $x>1$ and $y>1$. (This principle is very similar to Pauli's exclusion principle in Particle Physics.)

There are over 200 different primary U.P.'s, but the strength/intensity of each quality varies from one unit to infinite units. They can be distinguished simply as two basic types: effect U.P.'s or cause U.P.'s. Thus the whole universe is formed. Note that hard/soft and light/heavy have been excluded from the U.P.'s qualities because these are the qualities of the dense U.P.'s or their combinations. (The karmons are some of the finest particles formed from U.P.'s and therefore might be

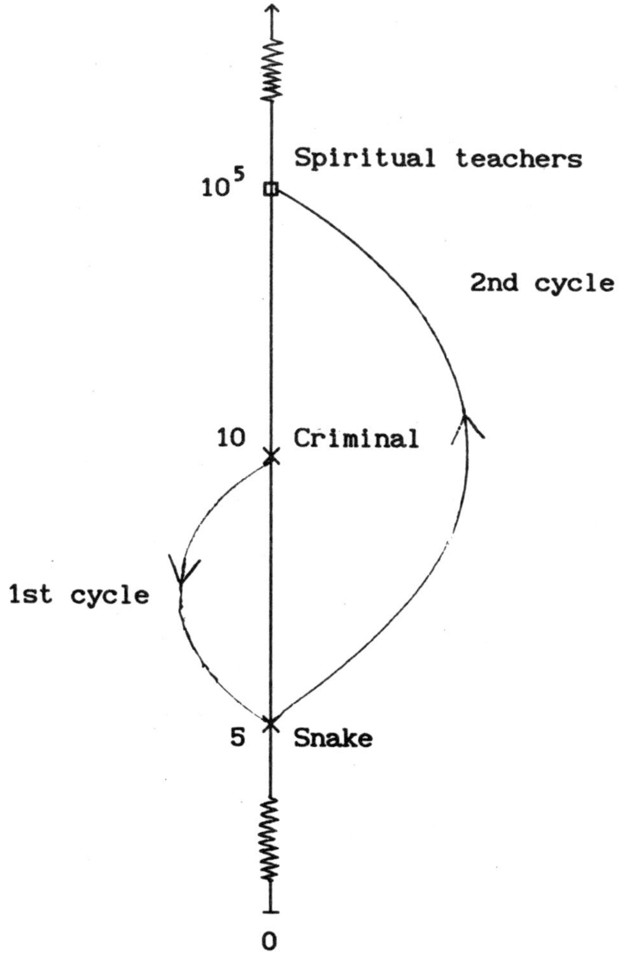

Fig. 4.4 Life-axis with two consecutive life-cycles depending on the karmic matter from a criminal to a snake in the first cycle and then to a spiritual teacher in the second cycle.

combinations of only two U.P.'s.)

4.6 PRACTICAL IMPLICATIONS OF CYCLES

It is quite clear that karmic matter plays a central role in shaping one's next incarnation along the life-axis (see, Ch. 2). Hence, an average human being indulging in criminal activities might end up in the next life as a snake because of the heavy karmic matter (see, Fig. 4.4). On the other hand, an average human being after expiation of his heavy karmic matter can go higher up the spiritual ladder, that is, he may be reborn with the karmic density, say of a *spiritual teacher*. The cycle continues: for example, the one who has become a snake could, after reducing karmic matter, again go higher as a human being in his second cycle, (see, Fig. 4.4). (It is possible for a snake to shed his heavy karmic matter; see the well-known Jain legend about a snake in Mahavira's life, Appendix 1.)

In view of Axiom 2, one can end the cycles only through the human state for which the karmic density is comparatively lower than for any other form of life. The methods of removing all the karmic matter in the human state, i.e. to finally cut the bonds that imprison the soul, will be given in the next chapter (see, Axiom 4A). However, when one's soul is liberated from the cycle of rebirth, it is stipulated that immediately another soul from a low form of life shoots higher; this leads in turn to souls in lower forms moving higher. Therefore, in liberating ourselves we are helping a lower life-form, etc. to rise up on the life-axis. This chain-like progression is an interesting concept.

4.7 GENERAL COMMENTS

The two important points assumed in Axiom 3, are (1) the science of mind and matter and (2) the theory of reincarnation. Pedler (1981) deals with the present trend amongst physicists to find laws which govern not only matter but also consciousness, i.e. to explain various phenomena such as metal bending, object moving, telepathy, etc. However, progress is limited in spite of great efforts. He describes those which are now at least being scientifically investigated. The work of Capra (1975) is definitely a step forward.

Regarding reincarnation, Wilson (1981) examines the

credibility of various reports of subjects who, under hypnosis, have apparently regressed into previous lives which they have described in realistic detail. He records that one Joe Keeton, a hypnotist, pronounces that there is no limbo, no rest between one life and another. From death to reincarnation is instantaneous. This hypothesis is precisely as given above.

4.8 GLOSSARY

1. Eight karmic components (=karma)
   A. Primary (= Ghātiyā)
   (a) Bliss-defiling = Mohanīya
   (a_1) Insight deluding = Darśana-Mohanīya
   (a_2) Conduct deluding = Cāritra-Mohanīya
   (b) Energy obstructing = Vīrya-antarāya
   (c) Knowledge obscuring = Jñāna-āvaraṇīya
   (d) Perception obscuring = Darśana-āvaraṇīya
   B. Secondary (= Aghātiyā)
   (e) Feeling producing = Vedanīya
   (e_1) Pleasure producing = Sātā-vedanīya
   (e_2) Pain producing = Asātā-vedanīya
   (f) Body producing = Nāma
   (g) Longevity determining = Āyu
   (h) Environmental determining = Gotra
2. Types of bodies (= Śarīra)
   Karmic body = Kārmic Śarīra
   Luminous capsule = Taijas Śarīra
3. Six Existents (= Dravya)
   (1) Soul = Jīva
   (2) Matter = Pudgala
   (3) Space = Ākāśa; occupied space = Loka Ākāśa; unoccupied space = Aloka-Ākāśa.
   (4) Dynamic medium = Adharma
   (5) Stationary medium = Dharma
   (6) Time = Kāla

Space point = Pradeśa
Ultimate Particle = Paramāṇu
Sub-atomic = Aṇu.
(Particle-Groupings variforms = Vargaṇā)

NOTES

1. P.S. Jaini, p. 125. Nāma-karmas pertaining to śarīra are also said to

generate two subtle bodies underlying the manifest physical one. These are the *taijasa-śarīra*, heat body, which maintains the vital temperature of the organism, and the *kārmana-śarīra*, the karmic body, constituting the sum total of karmic material present in the soul at a given time. The conception that such bodies exist is important to the Jain theory of rebirth, since they constitute the "vehicle" whereby a soul moves (albeit under its own power) from one incarnation to the next.

2. P.S. Jaini, pp. 126-7. At the moment of death, the *aghātiyā* karmas have pre-programmed, as it were, the particular conditions of the coming embodiment. This information is carried in the kārmana-śarīra, which together with the taijasa-śarīra, houses the soul as it leaves its physical body. A soul is said to be inherently possessed of great motive force; set free of the state of gross embodiment, it flies at incredible speed and in a straight line to the destination which its accompanying karma deemed appropriate. This movement is called vigraha-gati, and it is said to require, as noted above, only a single moment in time, regardless of the distance to be traversed.
3. P.S. Jaini, p. 98. The distinguishing quality of space is its ability to provide a locus for such existents; this is true whether it actually does so (as in the case of loka-ākāśa) or not (as in the case of aloka-ākāśa). Hence, there is only one "space"; its extent is infinite. Ākāśa is further described as divisible into infinitesimally small "space-points" (pradeśa); these units have some dimension and yet cannot be sub-divided.

5

PRACTICAL KARMIC FUSION (AXIOM 4A)

Axiom 4A : "*Karmic fusion is due to perverted views, non-restraint, carelessness, passions and activities.*"

5.1 THE AXIOM

WE KNOW from previous chapters that the density of karmic matter makes the difference between various species, and at the human level the density is small. However, to realise the full power of the soul it is important to remove the karmic matter. Before we try to find how this can be achieved at the human level it is important to understand how karmic fusion takes place in practice.

We now try to give practical ideas of the abstract themes developed in Chs. 2-4. The karmic force field is set up by the activities of the body, mind and speech or in short by Jain yoga, whereas the karmic fusion takes place due to the volitional activities of the individual, i.e. the exercise of one's own will. Note that activities in themselves, like a new born child who has no volition to do right and wrong, cannot set up a karmic force field and thus cannot attract karmons. However, when these volitional activities are performed, the karmons are attracted and fused.[1]

The axiom gives the five agents:

Perverted Views, Nonrestraint,
Carelessness, Passion and Activities,

which influence the karmic matter and its forces; we will call these the five karmic agents, each undermining the four soul-elements:—

Knowledge, Perception, Bliss and Energy.

The karmic agent, Perverted Views, means false notions regarding the nature of the soul or misunderstanding about

"Who am I?" In our context it will mean not believing in Axioms 1 to 3. Thus the knowledge and perception elements are obscured. The term Non-restraint implies there is no self-control which may lead to involuntary evil deeds. Thus, the bliss element is defiled. The term Carelessness implies general inertia in working towards mokṣa. Thus the Energy Element is obstructed. Jain Yoga refers to general activities of the body, mind and speech and should not be confused with the modern meaning of the word yoga. Positive Yoga (= sacred activities) leads to light karmic matter whereas Negative Yoga (= harmful activities) leads to heavy karmic matter (Appendix 3B, q. 5.1). The last of the agents responsible for karmic fusion is Passion. This is the main agent for fusion (Appendix 3B, q. 5.2), and it influences all the four soul elements which we will describe fully in § 5.3.

5.2 KARMIC COMPONENTS IN PRACTICE

We now describe the practical effect of each of eight types of karmic components defined in § 4.2. The Insight Deluding Component gives rise to false views including extremism and an inability to discriminate between what is proper and what is improper. The Conduct Deluding Component generates passions and sentiments which delude right conduct. These two sub-components act simultaneously to create a state of spiritual blockage. The Knowledge Obscuring Component obstructs knowledge in five ways. It obstructs (1) the function of the senses and mind, (2) logical ability, (3) clairvoyance power, (4) mind-reading ability, and (5) omniscience ability. The Perception Obscuring Component obstructs perception by means of eyes and other senses, perception before clairvoyance, perception related to omniscience. The Bliss Defiling Component (Insight Deluding and Conduct Deluding) limits the energy of the soul and activities of the body, mind and speech, and it creates confusion and desires which then allow other karmic components to be operative. Its effect is very much like the significant transformation of oneself taking place under intoxication.

We now summarise the secondary set of karmic components. The Feeling Producing Component characterises mental state.

The Body Producing Component determines the type of species, sex and colour. The Longevity Component determines longevity in the next birth. The Environmental Component determines the level of circumstances conducive to pursue spiritual life.

5.3 VOLITIONAL ACTIVITIES AND THE FOUR PASSIONS

We now give the details of the karmic dynamics in practice. Let x be the number of karmons involved in fusion due to a volitional activity. Note that the new karmic matter remains dormant for some time before the emission begins. Table 5.1 gives the four important factors related to the x karmons.

Table 5.1 *The life and activity of x-karmons involved in fusion with* $x_1 + \ldots + x_8 = x$ *

Karmic components	Quantity to each component	Time interval to decay	Strength in decay
a	x_1	$(t_1^{(1)}, t_1^{(2)})$	f_1
b	x_2	$(t_2^{(1)}, t_2^{(2)})$	f_2
c	x_3	$(t_3^{(1)}, t_3^{(2)})$	f_3
d	x_4	$(t_4^{(1)}, t_4^{(2)})$	f_4
e	x_5	$(t_5^{(1)}, t_5^{(2)})$	f_5
f	x_6	$(t_6^{(1)}, t_6^{(2)})$	f_6
g	x_7	$(t_7^{(1)}, t_7^{(2)})$	f_7
h	x_8	$(t_8^{(1)}, t_8^{(2)})$	f_8

(*See 'Notes' on page 51 for further details on notation.)

The precise number of karmons, x, in fusion depends upon the *degree of volition* with which the activity was carried out. The distribution of x over the different karmic components depends on the *type of activity*, i.e. the type of activity determines the specific karmic component taken up by the undifferentiated karmons. The time to decay and the corresponding potential strength of each component is fixed by the *degree of passions* with which the activity takes place. Once the karmon has had its effect, it is emitted from the soul, returning to an undifferentiated state and thus to the infinite pool of free karmons.[2] Note that the time of activation, duration of emission and the strength of each karmic component can be different. Also, it is possible to enforce premature decay, suppression of their effect, etc. through practical means (see, Ch. 7). Passion is the main agent for karmic fusion. It has four main sub-agents:

Anger, Pride, Deceit and Greed.

We will describe these as the Four (principal) Passions. They are depicted in Fig. 5.1. Note that gluttony and covetousness are both expressions of greed. The attraction of karmons is stronger on greed and deceit but weaker on anger and pride. However, both can occur simultaneously. Given a particular situation, the activities of body, mind and speech occur (Fig. 5.2a), activating the karmic field. Karmons are picked up and then attracted or repulsed by the Four Passions (Fig. 5.2a). The incoming karmons go through the process of fusion to the existing karmic matter (underlining the Four Passions for simplicity) through the energy element of the soul (Fig. 5.2b); this is one's personal reaction in view of the existing karmic matter. They are then assigned a function depending on subsequent volitional activity, i.e. a righteous action will lead to light karmic matter being added whereas an unrighteous action leads to heavy karmic matter being added (Fig. 5.2b), i.e. ending up with a weaker or stronger karmic fusion, respectively. Note how these processes compare in practice with those abstract processes described in Ch. 2. In particular, Fig. 5.2 is a practical representation of Fig. 2.1.

It should be noted that Anger and Pride are grouped as "Attachment" whereas Deceit and Greed are grouped as "Aversion" since these reflect such emotional states.

5.4 DEGREES OF PASSIONS

We may now illustrate the strength of the main passions—anger, pride, deceit and greed, assigning to them five degrees 0, 1, 2, 3, 4. Of course, these imply the proportional density of fusions of karmons, that is, the higher the degree, the larger is the fusion, longer is its time to decay, and stronger is the karmic force.

The degrees of anger, pride, deceit and greed of 0, 1, 2, 3, and 4 can be illustrated through (cf. Stevenson, 1915, p. 124) the following metaphors:

1. *Anger:* In the case of anger, Degree 1 is like a line drawn

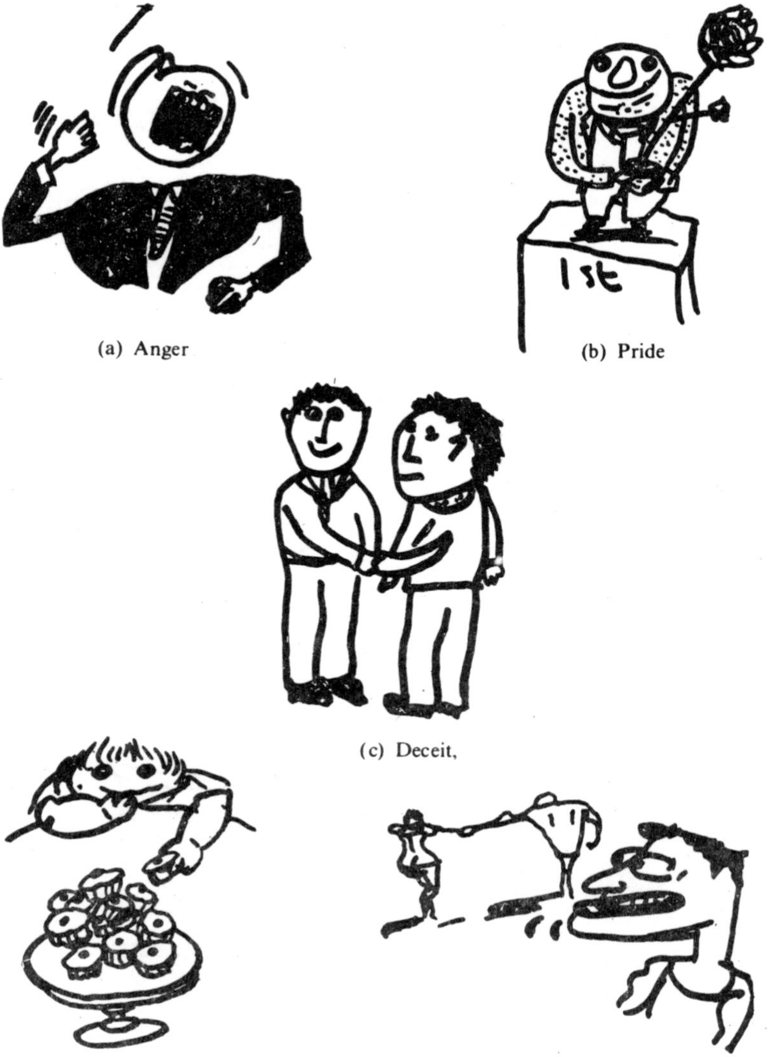

(a) Anger (b) Pride

(c) Deceit,

(d_1) Gluttony, (d_2) Covetousness.

Fig. 5.1 The Four Passions (principal) in Jainism.

with a stick on water which almost instantaneously passes away. Degree 2 is like a line drawn on a beach which the tide washes away. Degree 3 is like a ditch dug in a sandy soil which, after one year's weather, silts up. Degree 4, the worst of all, is like a deep crack in a mountain side which will remain until the end of time. Degree zero of anger implies serenity/tolerance.

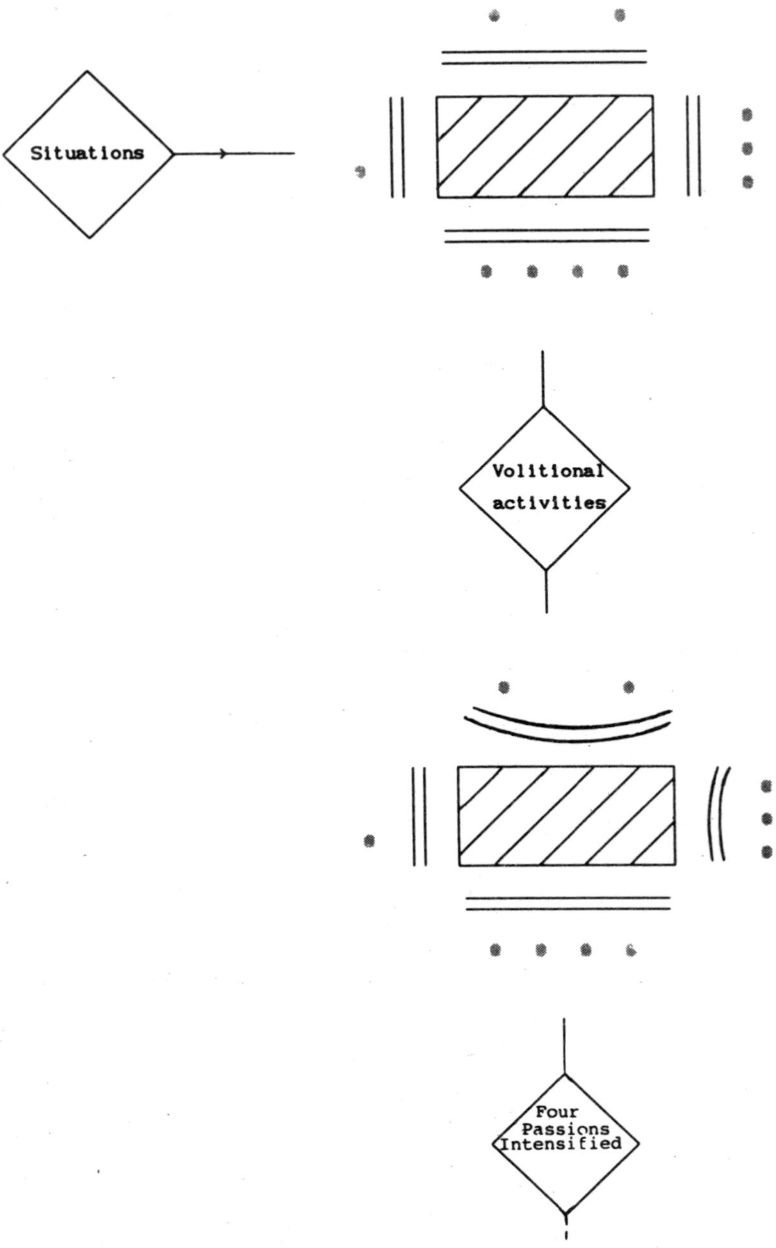

Fig. 5.2 A flowchart of the dynamics of karmic bondage shown in two parts: (a) situation and volitional activities with activated karmic force;

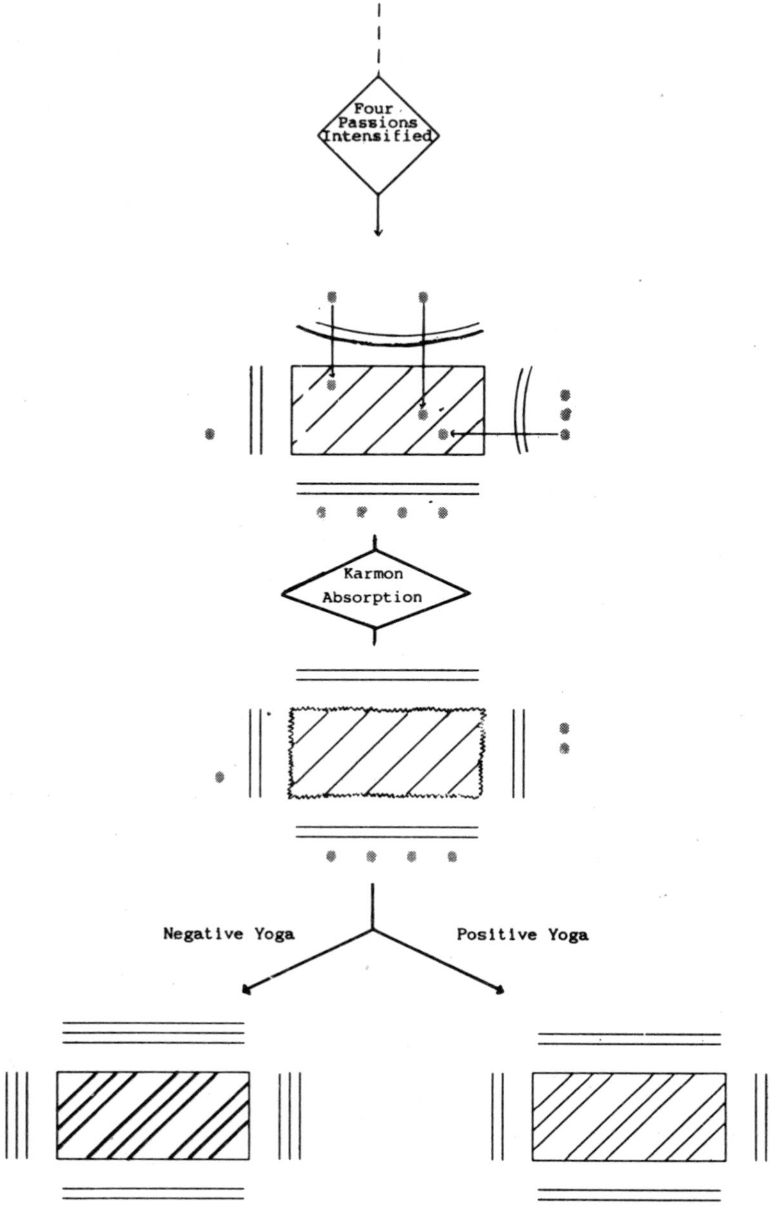

Fig. 5.2 (b) passions and yoga leading to karmic influx, karmic fusion and revised karmic matter.

2. *Pride:* We now illustrate the five degrees of pride. The first one is like a twig which is pliable and easily bent. The second degree is like a young branch of a tree which can be bent by a storm. The third degree is like beams of wood cut from a mature tree which may only be bent by being oiled and heated. Pride in the fourth degree, outdoes any analogy taken from a tree, being as unbending as a piece of granite. Degree zero of pride implies humility.

3. *Deceit:* Deceit can be compared to crookedness. In the first degree it can be straightened as one could straighten a stalk of wheat bent by the wind. In the second degree it is like the edge of a lawn which has been badly cut and requires much work to straighten it. In the third degree it is like a crooked tooth which once allowed to grow unchecked cannot be straightened. The fourth degree is like a knot in a tree. Degree zero indicates straightforwardness.

4. *Greed:* Greed is said to change the colour of the human heart. In the first degree it will stain the heart yellow like a water based paint that can be easily washed off with just water. In the second degree, the heart will be soiled like cooking pans full of fat which can only be cleaned with great labour. In the third degree, the stain is like the mark left by oil on clothing which is only removed after much dry-cleaning. In the fourth degree, it is like a permanent dye which cannot be removed. Degree zero of greed implies complete contentment and charitable attitude.

These degrees can be related to the lengths of the time periods for their effects to last (see, Glasenapp, 1942). Degree 4 of a major passion is of lifelong duration. Degree 3 of a major passion is of one year duration. Degree 2 of a major passion lasts 4 months. Degree 1 of a major passion is the level called smouldering passions and is of a fortnight duration. Degree zero of all major passions implies a higher spiritual state. Mehta (1939) has given a comprehensive treatment of Jain psychology, and in particular, has treated the doctrine of karmons and the four passions in the light of modern psychology.

We mentioned Four (principal) Passions—Anger, Pride, Deceit and Greed. In fact, these four are also responsible for quasi-passions or sentiments of nine kinds—namely laughter, pleasure, displeasure, sorrow, fear, disgust and sexual cravings for male/female and hermaphrodite. Worrying is included in "fear", etc. but more as a part of violence to oneself which is to be discussed in the next chapter.

5.5 GLOSSARY

1. Activities = Yoga
   Volition = Bhāva
2. *Five Karmic Agents*
   Perverted Views = Mithyādarśana
   Nonrestraint = Avirati
   Carelessness = Pramāda
   Four Passions (principal) = Kaṣāya
   anger = krodha, pride = māna, deceit = māyā,
   greed = lobha
   Activities = Yoga
3. Quasi-Passions (subsidiary) = No-Kaṣāya
   Attachment = Rāga
   Aversion = Dvesa

NOTES

1. P.S. Jaini, p. 112. "The energy quality, "perverted" by this impurity, produces vibrations (yoga), which bring about the influx (āsrava) of different kinds of material karma. The vibrations referred to here actually denote the volitional activities of the individual. Such activities can be manifested through either body, speech, or mind;...."

* "The quantities of different karmons in karmic components are denoted by $x_1, ..., x_8$ The corresponding time intervals of decays of $x_1,..., x_8$ are $(t_1^{(1)}, t_1^{(2)}), ..., (t_8^{(1)}, t_8^{(2)})$. Thus for the karmic component a, the decay process begins at the time $t_1^{(1)}$ and lasts until $t_1^{(2)}$ and so on. $f_1, ..., f_8$ are corresponding strengths of each component in decay. It is understood here that the decay process is uniformly constant within each component a, b, ..., h but can vary between the components".

2. P.S. Jaini, p. 113. "The precise amount (pradeśa) of karma that engulfs the soul after a given activity is said to depend upon the *degree of volition* with which that activity was carried out. The type of activity, moreover, determines the specific nature (prakṛti) assumed by the theretofore

undifferentiated karmic matter....As for the duration (*sthiti*) and result (*anubhava*) of given karmas—how long they will cling to the soul and what precise momentary effect they will eventually have upon it—these are fixed by the degree to which such passions (kaṣāya) as anger and lust coloured the original activity. Once a karma has given its result, it falls away (*nirjarā*) from the soul "like ripe fruit", returning to the undifferentiated state and thus to the infinite pool of "free" karmic matter;...."

6

EXTREME ABSORPTION OF KARMONS (AXIOM 4B)

Axiom 4B : "*Violence to oneself and others results in the formation of the heaviest new karmic matter, whereas helping others towards mokṣa with positive non-violence results in the lightest new karmic matter.*"

6.1 THE AXIOM

FROM THE PREVIOUS chapter we know the agents which make the karmic flow possible. In Ch. 5 we have also mentioned that under positive yoga, the karmons get converted into light karmic matter whereas under negative yoga, the karmons get converted into heavy karmic matter. Conversely, the emission of that light karmic matter leads to good fruits while the fusion of that heavy karmic matter leads to bad fruits, e.g. light karmic matter may provide a better environment for spiritual progress whereas heavy karmic matter may lead to a lower form of life in future cycles.

Now there arises the question of how one gathers the lightest or the heaviest karmic matter. The actions which are responsible for these two extremities of fusion are violence and non-violence respectively (see, Fig. 6.1). Here, the word violence is used broadly. One commits violence to oneself or to others through volitional activities of body, mind and speech, or by urging others to commit violence or by approving violence committed by others. Further, the term violence implies any action accompanied by the giving of pain and the heightening of passion. Of course, the term includes killing which is reprehensible not only for the suffering of the victims but more for the highest degree of passions which significantly strengthens the killer's karmic bondage.

(a)

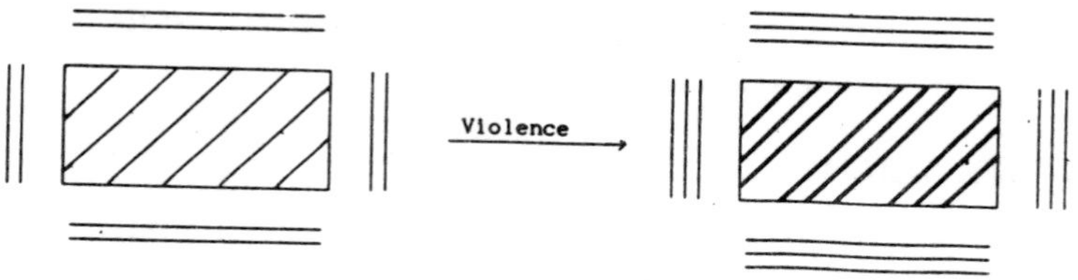

(b)

Fig. 6.1 Effect of (a) positive non-violence and (b) violence on the soul.

From Axiom 1 we are aware of the aspiration of all living beings to remove their karmic matter. Helping them towards this objective with dynamic non-violence rather than self-pity is positive non-violence. The intrinsic property of the soul is to "live and help others to live" (Appendix 3B, q. 6.1), i.e. the function of every soul is to gain mutual benefits by interacting with all others for the common good of spiritual advancement. Thus this Axiom encourages not only the aspirations of a single soul but, simultaneously, of all souls. However, the first responsibility is to oneself (i.e. love thyself), so that one is then capable of showing compassion, appreciation, etc. to others. The idea is emphasized in the quotation "You are your own best friend" (Appendix 3B, q. 6.2).

6.2 IMPLICATIONS

The idea of this Axiom lies in the belief that all living beings are sensitive to pain and no-one desires death (Appendix 3B, q. 6.3.). These remarks even apply to micro-organisms.

However, consuming any creature represented on the life-axis (see, Ch. 3) necessarily involves killing, so ideally it should be avoided.

For survival one has to consume food and thus we absorb life-units but the aim is to use the minimum possible number of life-units. The higher the spiritual growth, the lesser will be the total life units. In general, the consumption of life-units of 10^{-3} consisting of vegetable life, is regarded as tolerable. However, note that highly concentrated micro-organisms should be avoided since then the life-unit will be above 10^{-3}: this not only excludes honey and alcohol but also dead flesh as it is an ideal breeding ground for innumerable micro-organisms.[1] It also excludes tissues of certain plants hosting micro-organisms[2] (figs and tomatoes are taken as its symbolic representation). Of course, onions etc. are avoided since their life units are 10^{-2}. These represent minimizing violence by 'body' only.

The karmic matter which is taken in due to volitional activities affects the individual for a certain period of time only, the length of which depends on the type of action, degree of passion, motive etc. In fact, extreme forms of violence committed under perverted views could have an effect lasting for aeons, whereas if it is influenced by any of the Four Passions then the effect would not be quite so long-lasting. However, the duration of karmic matter in destroying only a one-sense life is very limited. The minimum times to karmic decay under Anger, Pride, Deceit and Greed are conventionally taken as 2 months, 1 month, a fortnight and less than 48 minutes respectively. Presumably an act of non-violence motivated by, say, greed may have this time decay. However, the maximum decay will be further reduced depending upon the weaker strength of the Four Passions. Of course, no karmic matter is absorbed during immobility (no-yoga) and therefore only the remaining karmic matter can be shed.

Implementation of positive non-violence requires full alertness in any action—physical, mental or through speech. Mahavira prefixed various discourses to his chief disciple Gautama (Appendix 3B, q. 6.4):

'Never to be careless even for a moment'.

It has four practical components: Amity, Compassion, Appreciation and Equanimity as described in the following quotation (Appendix 3B, q. 6.5):

> "To develop a feeling of amity towards all beings, a feeling of appreciation towards the meritorious, a feeling of compassion towards those in misery, and equanimity in instructing those who have lost the true values."

These ideas are expressed in an inspiring poem "Maitri Bhavanun" by Chitrabhanu which is now a well-known prayer (see, for example, Mardia, 1992).

As an analogy, it is like driving a car (a vehicle with tremendous power) towards one's destination. It is not only how you drive and what route you take, but carefulness plays a key role each second. We will come back to this analogy in Ch. 8.

Fig. 6.2 shows various situations in which violence and non-violence are manifested through activities of the body, speech and mind. It should be noted that (a) represents murder whereas (b) represents compassion, (c) represents extreme speech and (d) represents amity. For (e) the individual is thinking of fighting his enemy and for (f) the individual ponders on how he can help a friend (with an alcohol problem) with equanimity.

6.3 VOLITIONAL ASPECT OF VIOLENCE

As we have mentioned, thoughts as well as deeds, play an important role in forming heavy and light karmic matter. Thus one should exclude any deed involving "premeditated violence". However, such deeds should be contrasted with those which constitute "accidental/occupational violence". Thus the number of karmons assimilated by a surgeon even on the death of his patient under an intricate operation, is much less than that of a murderer. Further, the surgeon accumulates only light karmic matter (unless he is incompetent), whereas the murderer always accumulates the heaviest karmic matter.[3] An arable farmer kills insects accidentally in the course of his profession but he accrues mildly heavy karmic matter. Nevertheless, the use of insecticides and pesticides constitutes

Fig. 6.2 Situations illustrating how violence and corresponding positive non-violence occur through body [(a), (b)], speech [(c), (d)] and mind [(e), (f)] respectively.

destruction of life. In general, the concept of non-violence restricts occupations to those which do not involve premeditated destruction of life above 10^{-2} life units. Killing, even when done in the most extreme situation of self-defence —"defensive-violence", accrues heavier karmic matter.

For most individuals such drastic behaviour is rarely needed. A famous letter by Mahatma Gandhi to Raychand together with his answer highlights the spirit (see, for example, Mardia, 1992, pp. 14-15). However, the aim is to desist from performing or encouraging others in the premeditated or intentional destruction of souls embodied with two or more senses.

6.4 THE JAIN UNIVERSAL TEMPORAL CYCLES

Jains believe that the universe is finite and it contains various worlds supporting life, including human life. Each of these inhabited worlds goes through an endless series of cycles, half-progressive and half-regressive. However, their phases are different so that at every moment there is a living Tirthankara somewhere. These half-cycles are divided into six time-sections. We write m for misery and h for happiness.

For the regressive half cycle the successive time sections are:

(1) extremely happy, say hhh
(2) happy, hh
(3) more happy than unhappy, hhm
(4) more unhappy than happy, hmm
(5) unhappy, mm
(6) extremely unhappy, mmm.

We now enter the progressive half cycle where the successive time sections are:

(7) extremely unhappy, mmm
(8) unhappy, mm
(9) more unhappy than happy, mmh
(10) more happy than unhappy, mhh
(11) happy, hh
(12) extremely happy, hhh.

Note that (1) and (12), (2) and (11), etc. are similar. The cycles are represented in Fig. 6.3 and the area contained in each sector for m and h reflects the above ideas. Thus the full

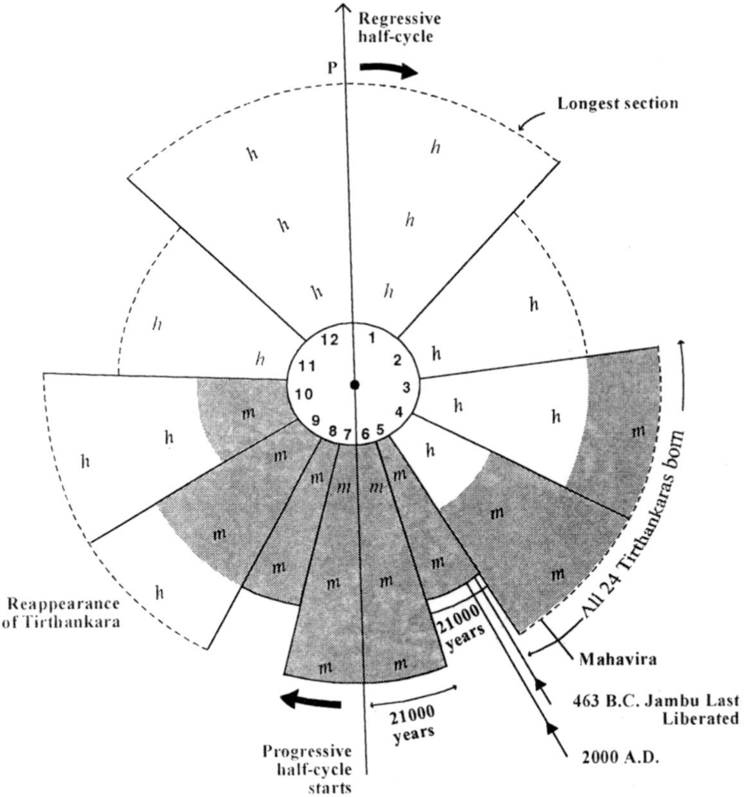

Fig. 6.3 One Jain universal temporal cycle (clock-wise) and circular histogram of the level of happiness and misery (*h* = happiness, *m* = misery, in shaded area); a broken arc indicates very large periods. The regressive half-cycle starts from the point P.

cycle, containing twelve time-sections, is:

(1)	(2)	(3)	(4)	(5)	(6)	(7)	(8)	(9)	(10)	(11)	(12)
hhh	hh	hhm	hmm	mm	mmm	mmm	mm	mmh	mhh	hh	hhh

We denote a full Jain Temporal Cycle by 1 J.T.C. We note the following points:

In Fig. 6.3, the time goes around clockwise. The periods in each section are very large. One of the smaller units is *sagarpomas,* 1 sagarpomas is at least 10^{17} J.T.C. In this unit, as we have described before, the duration of various karmic components is measured. The time-sections 5,6,7 and 8 are believed to be of 21,000 years each, others are vast but not infinite, and these are therefore represented by broken sector-lines. The time-sections and half cycles follow on from each other in a continuous and smooth manner. At the present time, we are 2,592 years (in 1996) into time-section 5 of the regressive half-cycle.

It is believed that only during time-sections (3, 4) or (7, 8) can one possibly be a Tirthankara/perfect being. All the twentyfour Tirthankaras of the present half-cycle (regressive) were born during the third (hhm) and fourth (hmm) sections. These combinations of h and m are necessary and sufficient to pursue the course of self-realization. We are now 2,592 years (in 1996) into the fifth time-section of 21,000 years so that it will be a long while before any more Tirthankaras/perfect beings emerge on this earth. However, spiritually higher persons can contact a Tirthankara in other worlds as there is always one Tirthankara somewhere in the universe at any instant.[4]

Jambu, one of the disciples of Sudharman (see Appendix 2) is assumed to be the last person in the present time cycle to reach mokṣa on earth, about 463 B.C. A verse of the scripture Kalpasutra (v. 146) describes when Mahavira instituted the fifth section of the time cycle mm; Jacobi (1884, p. 269) describes this verse as a 'rather dark passage' in Kalpasutra for obvious reasons.

6.5 GLOSSARY

1. *Violence* (= Hiṃsā)
   Non-violence/harmlessness = Ahiṃsā
   Premeditated violence = Saṃkalpajā-hiṃsā
   Accidental/occupational violence= Ārambhajā-hiṃsā
   Defensive violence = Virodhi-hiṃsā
2. *Temporal Cycles* (= Kāla)
   Progressive half-cycle = Utsarpiṇī
   Regressive half-cycle = Avasarpiṇī
   Happy = Suṣamā
   Misery/unhappy = Duṣamā

NOTES

1. P.S. Jaini, p. 169 "...the dead flesh itself is a breeding ground for innumerable nigodas and hence must not be consumed."
2. P.S. Jaini, p. 168. "Such creatures (nigodas) are said to be especially prevalent in substances where fermentation or sweetness is present; hence the consumption of liquor or honey brings untold millions of these organisms to an untimely and violent end. The tissues of certain plants, especially those of a sweet, fleshy, or seed-filled nature, are also thought to serve as hosts for nigoda; plants of this type are termed sādhārana, 'those which share their bodies'. The avoidance of figs as part of the mūlaguṇa practice seems to represent a symbolic renunciation of all nigoda-ridden vegetable substances;..."
3. P.S. Jaini, p. 171. "A murderer, for example, clearly sets out to end the life of his victim, hence commits saṃkalpajā-hiṃsā. Surgeons, on the other hand, may cause pain or even death during a delicate operation, but are guilty only of the much less serious ārambhajā-hiṃsā."
4. P.S. Jaini, p. 32 "...at every moment there is a living Jina somewhere. In other words the path of salvation is open at any time; one need only be born into one of the Videhas in order to have an immediate chance for mokṣa."

7
THE PATH TO SELF-CONQUEST (AXIOM 4C)

Axiom 4C: *"Austerity forms the karmic shield against new karmons as well as setting off the decaying process in the old karmic matter."*

7.1 THE AXIOM

FROM AXIOMS 4A and 4B we know how karmons flow in. However, from previous chapters it is clear that the general aim is two-fold, (1) to stop the inflow of new karmons through the karmic shield and (2) to completely emit the old karmic matter. If these objectives can be achieved then one will be left with pure soul with its full power, namely, its infinite energy, absolute bliss, and perfect knowledge and perception as described in Ch. 2.

It is expected that the full power of the soul can only be achieved by removing the effects of the karmic matter revealed in practical terms by the volitional activities of body, mind and speech. As we have seen, these are the external functions which continuously act and react in the karmic field as reactions in a nuclear reactor. Further, there is a sort of personal karmic computer attached which keeps an up-to-date record and manages instructions in real time. The question arises as to how one can remove karmic matter as well as stop further karmic fusion. Rationally, one's slavery to the dictates of one's lower nature should be part of karmic matter since it checks the soul from having its full power. Hence, it is only some form of austerity or restraint that can check the inflow of karmons, i.e. austerity is the only way by which one is able to escape from constraints of one's physical nature and psyche which are under the continuous influence of the karmic field (see, Fig. 7.1). Also, this Axiom advocates austerity as a way of eliminating the five karmic agents of Axiom 4A, viz., perverted views, non-

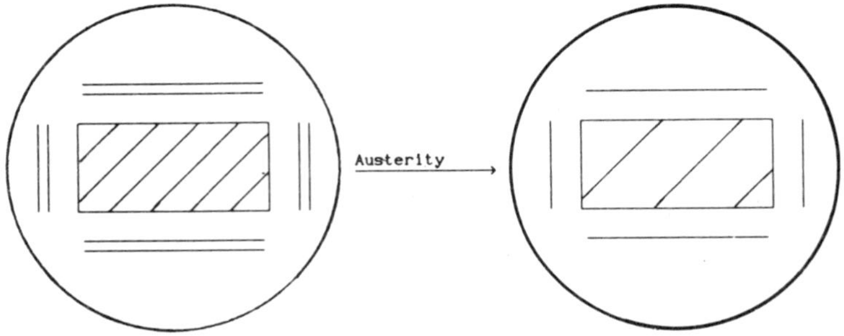

Fig. 7.1 Karmic force shield (circle) and karmic emission (less diagonal lines) through austerity.

restraint, carelessness, passions and activities. The process of the gradual elimination of these karmic agents can be presented in "fourteen purification stages" which we describe below.

Austerities should be understood in a wider context. They imply the control of the senses with extreme alertness while keeping positive non-violence in the forefront. That is, "Exert yourself according to your capacity" (Appendix 3B, q. 7.1), which means that one should not practise austerities to the extent of harming oneself by trying to go beyond one's capabilities. It should never be confused with masochism.

7.2 PURIFICATION AXIS AND FOURTEEN PURIFICATION STAGES

We have already introduced the life axis in Ch. 3. Now we come to the upper portion relevant to human beings who are already spiritually higher than other life forms. The purification axis plots the human beings from those with low life units to those with very high life units, i.e. with maximum karmic density to those who have the lowest karmic density. In other words, it is the upper part of the life-axis which has been extended. This is described as the ladder one must climb as one progresses from heavy karmic density to a very low quantity of karmic matter and eventually to liberation.

This ladder has fourteen rungs which are stages of spiritual purification. We will call these the *fourteen purification stages.* The higher one is on the ladder, the higher is the degree of purification (*or Jainness*) and the lesser is the karmic matter. Fig. 7.2 shows the purification axis with the names of the stages.

The first point shown on the axis is the first rung applicable

14	Static omniscience state
13	Dynamic omniscience state
12	C.S.R. with eliminated greed
11	C.S.R. with suppressed greed
10	C.S.R. with subtle greed
9	C.S.R. with uniformly mild volition
8	Complete self-restraint (C.S.R.) with unprecedented volition
7	Carelessness-free self-restraint (S.R.)
6	E.W.V. with careless self-restraint (S.R.)
5	E.W.V. with partial self-restraint (S.R.)
4	Non-restrained enlightened world-view (E.W.V.)
3	Mixture of deluded and enlightened world-view (E.W.V.)
2	Lingering enlightened world-view (E.W.V.)
1	Deluded world-view

Purification stage

Fig. 7.2 Purification axis with fourteen stages. (E.W.V. = Enlightened World-View, S.R. = Self-Restraint, C.S.R. = Complete Self-Restraint)

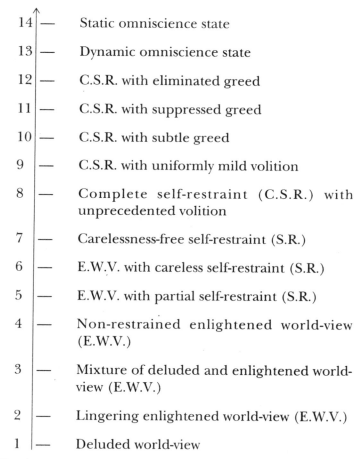

to all beings and it is here that the karmic matter is at its densest for human beings. The karmic matter decreases up the ladder and is zero at the 14th rung. Thus inversely, we could view the purification axis as through the karmic density axis with fourteen important points on it—the karmic density axis being continuous.

To understand the dynamic process of karmic fission, it should be clearly understood that as karmons are shed, there is an increase in the energy of the soul which allows further spiritual growth. It is assumed that future karmic influx will be checked, and there will be a further release of energy and knowledge elements which allows the soul to search for its true nature. Another important point to note is that the effect of the karmic matter is mostly first suppressed rather than altogether eliminated. Furthermore, each stage severely limits karmic fusion and diminishes old karmic matter, and at most of the stages the degrees of Anger, Pride, Deceit and Greed are reduced gradually, with Anger being the first to be reduced and so on. The five degrees of the Four Passions have already been described in Ch. 5. However, the overall aim is to eradicate all the five important agents of karmic fusion given in Axiom 4A.

7.3 FIRST FOUR STAGES

The first four stages in Fig. 7.2 are Deluded World-View (of reality), Lingering Enlightened World-View, Mixture of Deluded and Enlightened World-View and Non-Restrained Enlightened World-View (True-Insight) respectively.

7.3.1 *Definition of stages and internal motion*

The first rung of the ladder corresponds to all living beings with a Deluded World-View. In the beginning every soul is in this stage of complete ignorance, i.e. it has the Four Passions at the maximum level. However, in view of Axiom 1, every soul strives to release its four elements from karmic matter. This process can be triggered off by either internal experience such as remembering past lives or external experiences such as hearing the Jain teachings.[1] This event is followed in a flash by passing through stages 2 and 3 (defined below) to stage 4 which corresponds to "Non-Restrained Enlightened World-View." This experience is the complete revelation of the true nature of life and the reality of the soul, i.e. True Insight.

This first experience of True Insight lasts only for a few moments and it comes from jamming the insight-deluding karmic component rather than from its elimination. The jammed component will be quickly unjammed and will assert its influence again. Hence the soul will revert to its extreme perverted stage with all five karmic agents—Perverted Views, Non-restraint, Carelessness, Passions and Activities—operating with full force. However during this fall, the soul goes through the third purification stage for a short time where the gross passions remain suppressed but there is no longer True Insight; this stage is described as the stage of Mixture of Enlightened World-View. Below this is stage 2, the Lingering Enlightened World-View stage, in which the fourth degree of passions reassert themselves and instantaneously drop the soul down to stage-1 again. In the first transition to the fourth stage, the insight deluding component is suppressed only, but in subsequent (guaranteed) transitions, of longer durations, there is also partial elimination of this component. After a number of such transitions involving partial elimination-cum-suppression, the soul gets firmly established in the fourth stage to proceed to the fifth stage and beyond as it is described below. Table 7.1 is a summary of these stages.

Table 7.1 *List of the first four purification stages and the corresponding status*

Stage	Name	Status
1	Deluded World-View	Perverted state
2	Lingering Enlightened World-View	
3	Mixture of Deluded and Enlightened World-View	
4	Non-Restrained World-View	First step to purification

7.3.2 *Description of the fourth stage and visible signs*

At the fourth stage Perverted Views are removed and equanimity is attained. It is this increase in purity which allows the flash of True Insight to take place. The removal of the 4th degree of the Four Passions leads to increased energy and knowledge elements of the soul, which makes the soul search for true knowledge more vigorously than before. Also it places significantly less emphasis on the manifestation of karmic matter including on one's own body, psychological states seen through the Four Passions and one's personal possession to which it had formerly identified itself.[2] Thus, a pure and serene state is attained.

Attitude and Inner-self

By now, one's serene state encourages an attitude which wishes to address the question "Who am I?" This attitude exerts the perception element of the soul even further and, through a surge of the energy element not before experienced, further removal of karmic matter takes place. Permanent attainment of True Insight is now possible. One becomes aware of the truth of the first three axioms. An aim to remove the effect of karmic forces is thus created and this desire leads to a further release of the energy element. All obstructions to insight are thereby prevented from exerting any influence and at that moment the soul experiences a permanent view of reality.

The internal sign of Enlightened World-View due to the Four Passions being limited to the third degree is self-transformation. The attention of the soul is deliberately reorientated, coming to focus upon nothing but its own true nature. Thus identification with the true inner-self, as opposed to 'I', is achieved, and the bliss element is now deeply experienced.

Behaviour and Positive Non-Violence[3]

Being at peace with oneself leads to sublime and relaxed behaviour. One is aware of the fundamental similarities of all living beings and this feeling of togetherness generates amity towards all and great compassion for the less fortunate. This *compassion* is free from pity and free from any personal ties with a particular being. Due to this realisation the soul recognises that all creatures are potential candidates for liberation. There is an unselfish longing to help other souls towards liberation with equanimity. Positive non-violence causes the evils of exploitative and destructive behaviour to be recognised. This aspect of positive non-violence is the practical application of Axiom 4B.

Effects on the Four Passions

In order to reach the fourth stage, austerities are not mentioned explicitly anywhere, but implicitly it is assumed that they are required since, to be in the fourth purification stage, one has to have all the degrees of the Four Passions down to level three which cannot be achieved without restraint. In any case, non-violence cannot occur without self-restraint.

The first awakening removes some of the karmons leading to a moderate degree of self-control/restraint, i.e. one does not get into a fit of anger, intriguing deceit, blinding pride, devouring greed etc. Further, on the perfection of the fourth purification stage, there will be evidence of more tolerance and less anger, more humility and less pride, more straightforwardness and less deceit, more contentment and less greed.

7.4 STAGE FIVE TO STAGE ELEVEN

As already seen in § 7.3, when perverted views are replaced by True Insight one rises to the fourth stage. At the fifth stage one starts working to achieve even greater restraint; that is, one follows various vows that lead to partial restraint. At the sixth stage, full restraint is accomplished.

The fifth stage is equivalent to the way of life of the ordinary layman whereas the sixth stage corresponds to following the path of a monk. At stage six, i.e. at the state of full restraint, full discipline and higher vows are achieved. How these various stages are achieved is described in Ch. 8.

At stage seven, one removes Carelessness to zero, implying also that Anger goes to zero and therefore this stage is called the Carelessness-free Self-Restraint stage. However, some remnants of the Four Passions still persist. At stages eight, nine and ten one tries through meditation to decrease the degree of Pride, Deceit and Greed to the zeroth degree respectively. The eighth, ninth and tenth stages of meditational attainment are: Complete Self-Restraint with (8) Unprecedented Volition (9) Uniformly Mild Volition and (10) Subtle Greed respectively. Table 7.2 summarises the details of these stages.

When in these states, if the Four Passions are suppressed rather than eliminated, then one will only be able to reach the eleventh stage called the Complete Self-Restraint with

Table 7.2 *List of the fifth to eleventh purification stages and the corresponding status (E.W.V. =Enlightened World-View, S.R. =Self-Restraint, C.S.R. =Complete S.R.)*

Stage	Name	Status
5	E.W.V. With Partial S.R.	True Jain Layman
6	E.W.V. With Careless S.R.	Monk
7	Carelessness Free S.R.	Spiritual Teacher
8	C.S.R. With Unprecedented Volition	Spiritual Masters
9	C.S.R. With Uniformly Mild Volition	Advanced Masters
10	C.S.R. With Subtle Greed	
11	C.S.R. With Suppressed Greed	Passionless State

Suppressed Greed State from which one will be forced to move downwards. However, if the Four Passions and their effects are fully eliminated during the trances, so that the degree of greed becomes permanently zero, then one will jump straight from the tenth stage to the twelfth stage—the "Complete Self-Restraint with Eliminated Greed" state.

7.5 LEVELS TWELVE TO FOURTEEN

On the instant of attaining the twelfth stage, three remaining primary karmic components (other than Deluding Karmic Component) are automatically eliminated, leading to the attainment of the thirteenth stage which is the state of omniscience and will be called the "Dynamic Omniscience State". At this stage only yoga governs the remaining activities which are necessary for the physical body to still function. These activities do not, however, lead to new karmons. Also, secondary karmic components of the omniscient being gradually fall off until eventually none of them remain. In the final moments, the body is in a state of total immobility—this state is the "Static Omniscience" stage and is the fourteenth stage.[4] This state lasts only for at the most 48 minutes prior to mokṣa. The moment death occurs, the soul, completely and forever freed from the cycle of rebirth, attains mokṣa. Table 7.3 summarises these details for these higher stages.

Note that stage four is the attainment of "Non-restrained Enlightened World-View"; stage five is attainment of the household state of lower vows; stage six is the attainment of a saintly level of higher vows; stage seven is very much like the

Table 7.3 *List of the final three purification stages and their status*

Stage	Name	Status
12	Completely Self-Restraint with Eliminated Greed	
13	Dynamic Omniscience state	Tirthankara
14	Static Omniscience state	Towards Moksa

state of a spiritual teacher; stages eight to ten are those of spiritual masters; stages twelve and thirteen are stages of Tirthankara/Dynamic Omniscience. The fourteenth stage is the state of omniscience at the instant prior to mokṣa. These stages can be approximately correlated with different personality profiles. Stage 1 is marked by primitive personality, stage 2 represents regression to primitive personality from higher stages, and stage 3 relates to confused personality. Stages 4, 5, 6 can be ascribed to solid, refined and sublime personalities respectively. In stage 7, the sublime personality also has the hall-mark of extreme alertness. All higher stages denote various levels of transcendental personalities.

7.6 SCHEMATIC REPRESENTATIONS OF THE LEVELS AND TRANSITIONS

It will be useful to express these ideas quantitatively. Recall from Ch. 5, that we have the five degrees 0, 1, 2, 3, 4 for each of the Four Passions. The following question arises—how can one assign the degrees to the other karmic agents? Remembering from Ch. 6 that violence through Perverted Views can last for 3½ J.U.C. (Jain universal cycle) in relation to 2 J.U.C. for any of the Four Passions. Thus, we give a nominal scale of 0 to 7 to the characteristic Perverted Views. Taking this point further, we can assign a maximum score of 4 to Non-restraint, 4 to Carelessness, 4 to Subsidiary Passions and 1 to Activities. Thus at stage 1, we have a total karmic density of 36 units. Working in this way for each stage, we can assign karmic densities which are presented in Table 7.4 together with some comments. However, these scores and scales are very arbitrary, and their function is only to give some insight into the gradual progression.

Fig. 7.3 gives a schematic representation of Table 7.4 at a finer scale. Along the x-axis are the Karmic Agents, and

Table 7.4 *The karmic density of karmic agents at different stages*

KEY Perverted Views = PV, Non-restraint = Nr, Carelessness = C, Anger =A, Pride = P, Deceit = D, Subsidiary Passions = SP, Greed = G and Activities = Ac. Total karmic density is the sum of the densities for PV, Nr,......, G and Ac.

				Passions							
Stage	PV	Nr	C	A	P	D	SP	G	Ac	Total Karmic Density	Comments
1	7	4	4	4	4	4	4	4	1	36	
2	5	4	4	4	4	4	4	4	1	34	
3	3	4	4	4	4	4	4	4	1	32	
4	0	4	4	3	3	3	3	3	1	24	Correct View achieved
5		2	4	2	2	2	2	2	1	17	
6		0	2	1	1	1	1	1	1	8	Full Restraint achieved
7			0	0	1	1	1	1	1	5	Watchfulness achieved, A= 0
8					0	1	1	1	1	4	Pride zero
9						0	1	1	1	3	Deceit zero
10							0	0.5	1	1.5	Subsidiary Passions removed
11								0.1	1	1.1	Very low Greed
12								0	1	1.0	Passions removed
13									0.1	0.1	Knowledge perfected
14									0.01	0.01	Activities stopping

along the y-axis is the level of spiritual purification. The karmic density should be looked at in a negative way, that is as the purity increases the karmic density decreases, i.e. the effect of the Four Passions becomes less. The karmic density has been represented by the z-axis parallel to the y-axis. By stage six, restraint has been fully accomplished and the total of the degrees of Anger, Pride, Deceit and Greed has dropped to eight. Following the lines from B to B' and C to C' we find that the values for Carelessness and Anger have become zero, although some degrees of the other three principal passions still remain.

In Fig. 7.3, it is worthwhile to note that there are separate boundaries for each of the agents, since there is no continuity, say, between perverted views and passions or even with the four Passions and nine Subsidiary Passions (= Quasi-Passions). The dissolution of every activity of the karmic agents starts as soon as the boundary line begins to become 'inclined', that

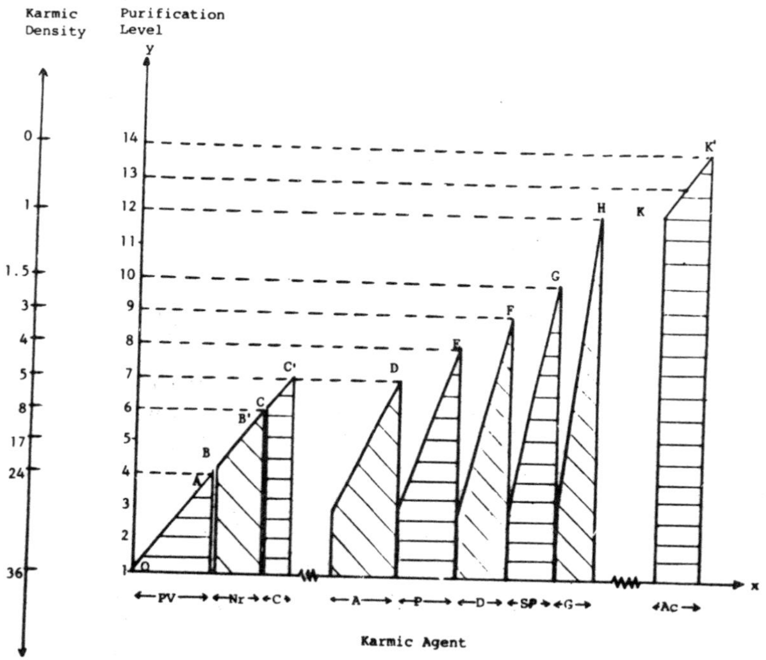

Fig. 7.3 Reduction in the karmic density and increase in the purification level; Perverted Views (=PV), Non-restraint (=Nr), Carelessness (=C), Anger (=A), Pride (=P), Deceit (=D), Greed (=G), Subsidiary Passions (=SP) and Activities (=Ac). The intercept of the line y = Constant, with the shaded figures represents the corresponding karmic density of the agents, when the base lengths at y = 1 are 7, 4, 4,...4, and 1 for PV, Nr, A,.., G and Ac, respectively.

is, with the emergence of triangular shapes. Thus point 0 represents the beginning of the removal of Perverted Views, but A becomes the point of the correct views of Table 7.4. The Non-restraint begins to be removed at point B, and by the time one reaches point B', there is Full Restraint or Discipline. Similarly, point C' is the point of Carefulness which is achieved at stage seven. D is the point of No Anger, that is, tranquility. E is the point of No Pride, that is, humility. F is the point of No Deceit, that is, straightforwardness/ simplicity; G is the point of No Subsidiary Passions. H is the point of No Greed, that is, contentment; and K is the point

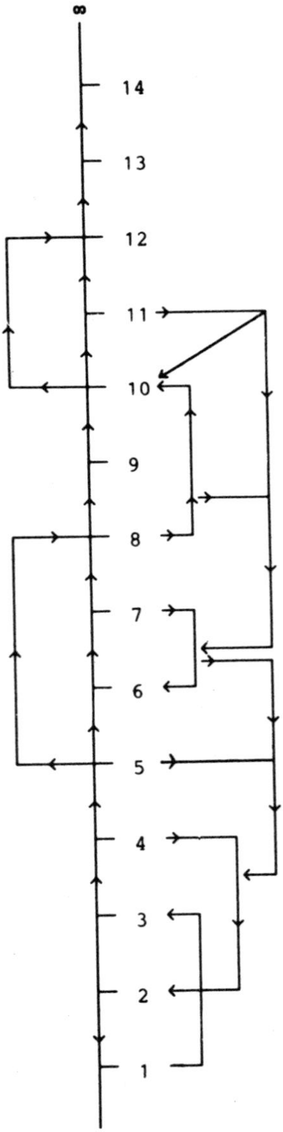

Fig. 7.4 Transitions on the purification axis; stage 2 is only possible through from the fall from stage 4 onwards.

just prior to mokṣa. It is to be observed that at the point K', that is, at stage thirteen, cessation of activity starts.

From Fig. 7.3, we can assess the karmic density to a finer value. For the first stage, we have y = 1 and from Table 7.4, the karmic density due to the Perverted Views (PV), Non-restraint (Nr),..., Greed (G) and Activities (Ac) are 7, 4,....... 4 and 1 units respectively. To find the karmic density at stage 5, we note that the line y = 5 does not intercept the triangle for PV so that the karmic density for PV is zero whereas at BB', the intercept at the trapezium is ½ the 'base' length of 4 so that the karmic density for Nr is 2. These are as in Table 7.4, but for G the intercept is not the half-length of the base of the corresponding trapezium as required in Table 7.4, but has karmic density slightly more than 2. Thus it is a continuous version of the 'step function' in Table 7.4.

Note that the life-units 10, 10^2, 10^3, 10^5, 10^{10}, 10^{100} of Ch. 3 correspond roughly to these karmic density units of 36, 24, 8, 5, 3, and 0.01 respectively.

7.7 TRANSITIONS BETWEEN STAGES

We have indicated how the transfer takes place from one stage to another. Fig. 7.3 shows the various transitions. The first part is the spiritual axis. From stage 1, we go into stage 3 then 4 and then either progress to stage 5 or fall back to stage 2, as indicated in Fig. 7.4. Again from stage 5, either we proceed to stage 6 or we go down to stage 4 or 2. From 6 we proceed to 7 or again we fall down to 5 or 4. From 7 we proceed to 8 or, as at 6, we go down. From 8 one can proceed to 9 or again we can go down. From 9, transition to 10 is possible. One can jump straight from 10 to 12. Stage 11 is very slippery and one can go downward anywhere, usually to 6 or 7. Once one has reached stage 12, then there is no fall and one progresses to stages 13 and 14. Appendix 4 gives a modified game of snakes and ladders to illustrate the most significant transitions.

7.8 GLOSSARY

Fourteen purification stages (= *Guṇasthānas*)

W.V.=World-View, E.W.V.= Enlightened World-View, S.R. = Self-Restraint, C.S.R.= Complete Self-Restraint.

Stage

1 Deluded W.V. = Mithyādṛṣṭi
2 Lingering E.W.V. = Sāsvādana
3 Mixture of Deluded and Enlightened W.V. = Mishra
4 Non-Restrained E.W.V. = Avirat Ṣamyak-dṛṣṭi
5 E.W.V. with Partial S.R. = Deśa-virata
6 E.W.V. with Careless S.R. = Pramatta-virata
7 Carelessness-Free S.R. = Apramatta-virata
8 C.S.R. With Unprecedented Volition = Apūrva-karaṇa
9 C.S.R. With Uniformly Mild Volition = Anivṛtti-Sāmparāya
10 C.S.R. With Subtle Greed = Sukṣma-moha
11 C.S.R. With Suppressed Greed = Upasanta-moha
12 C.S.R. With Eliminated Greed = Kṣīṇa-moha
13 Dynamic Omniscience State = Sayoga-kevalin
14 Static Omniscience State= Ayoga-kevalin

NOTES

1. P.S. Jaini, pp. 140-1. "....thanks to the fluctuations in the ongoing interaction of vīrya and karma, certain experiences (especially an encounter with a Jina or his image, hearing the Jaina teachings, or remembering past lives) *may* bring the bhavyatva out of its dormant state and thus initiate the process that leads eventually to mokṣa."
2. P.S. Jaini, p. 147. "Previously he has identified his being in external signs of life—the body, states, possessions; thus he has been in the state known as *bahirātman,* seeing the self in externals dominated by the consciousness which is aware only of the results of karma (*karma-phala-cetanā*)...... This orientation depends on the false notion that one can be the agent (*kartā*) of change in other beings;...."
3. P.S. Jaini, p. 150. "This awareness of the basic worth of all beings, and of one's kinship with them, generates a feeling of great compassion (*anukampā*) for others. Whereas the compassion felt by an ordinary man is tinged with pity or with attachment to its object, anukampā is free of such negative aspects; it develops purely from wisdom, from seeing the substance (dravya) that underlies visible modes, and it fills the individual with an unselfish desire to help other souls towards mokṣa."
4. P.S. Jaini, p. 159. "In the last few moments of embodiment, even yoga is brought to cessation; this state of utter immobility is called omniscience

without activities (*ayoga-kevalin*), the fourteenth guṇasthāna. At the instant of death (nirvāṇa) itself, the soul is freed forever from the last vestige of sāṁsāric influence;...."

8
THE PURIFICATION PRESCRIPTION

8.1 INTRODUCTION

In the last chapter, we described austerities as the antidote to the five karmic agents, Perverted Views, Non-restraint, Carelessness, Passions and Activities. In fact, the term austerities (according to Umasvati, see Appendix 3A, q. 8.1) implies the development of

> Restraint, Watchfulness, Righteousness, Reflection, Affliction-Mastery and Right Conduct.

Thus, there are 6 antidotes to the 5 karmic agents responsible for the stoppage of karmic influx and dissociation of karmic matter. However, all these 6 antidotes can be regarded as austerities by Axiom 4C.

We now describe in detail these 6 antidotes in relation to the fourteen purification stages. The above antidotes take up to the sixth stage once the basic foundation is laid down. The important point to bear in mind is that the prescription consists mainly of purifying the body through fasting, limiting speech through silence, and stilling the mind through meditation.

8.2 EIGHT QUALITIES OF TRUE-INSIGHT

Once the fourth stage of 'True-Insight' is attained, there are eight qualities of True Insight that arise before one can rise to a higher stage on the purification axis. Four of these qualities are of a negative nature. These are (1) Freedom from Doubts—regarding Jain teaching, (2) Freedom from Anticipation—regarding speculation about the future, (3) Freedom from disgust—arising from making a distinction between a pair of opposites, and (4) Freedom from False Notions— regarding gods, gurus and religious practices. The other four qualities are of a positive nature. These are (5) Safeguarding—the Jain faith from public criticism, by dealing with the failings of a fellow Jain through discreet instruction, (6) Promoting Stability—by making others more certain of their religious conviction when they are sceptical, (7) Illumination—by positive actions which promote the Jain religion. The last quality is (8) Disinterested Love which involves a selfless devotion to the ideal of mokṣa and thus great devotion to the monks pursuing this goal.

8.3 FIFTH STAGE FOR JAIN LAYMEN

Stage 5 involves the following eleven model steps of renunciation for laymen. This sub-ladder is shown in Fig. 8.1. The most important stage is the taking of the Lower Vows prescribed for a layman. Of these, the five Lower Vows are the

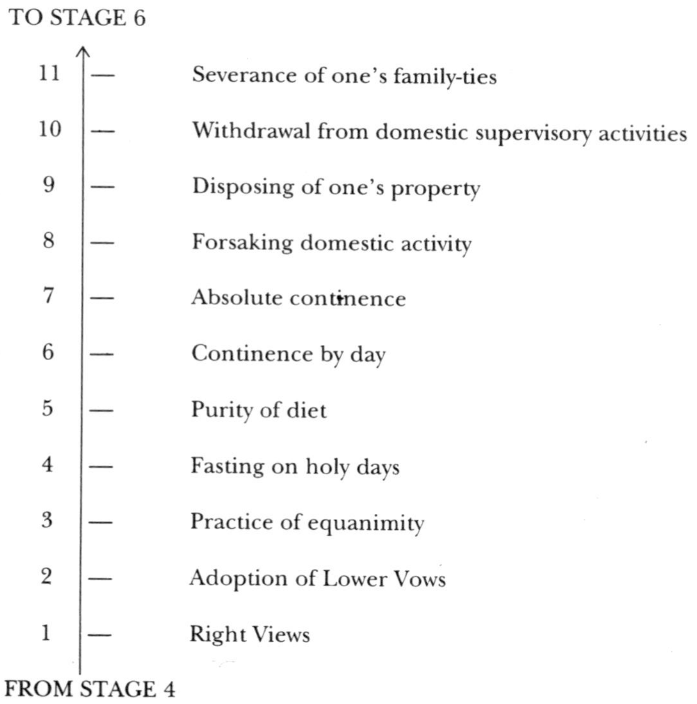

Fig. 8.1 The eleven model steps of renunciation for a layman associated with the fifth stage of purification.

most important. These are (a) avoiding injuring beings having two or more senses, (b) being truthful, (c) refraining from stealing, (d) not having sexual activities outside marriage, and (e) limiting one's possessions. Some additional vows help to strengthen and complement these lower vows. For details, see P.S. Jaini (1979, p. 187) and Williams (1963).

This last of the eleven sub-stages culminates in preparation for the next stage, that of the monk.

8.4 STAGE SIX AND MONKS

Stage 6 involves following Higher Vows which involve tougher austerities. These are extensions and additions to the Lower Vows (a)—(e) above and, in particular, include total renunciation of one's possessions, and ending domestic life altogether.

The overall aim is to minimize the extent and the frequency of activities which would lead to additional karmic matter being taken in through the arousal of new passions. We now describe in detail the practices required of a monk. These are meant to prepare an aspirant for the advanced meditational states through which karmic matter is finally eliminated from the soul, so that mokṣa is achieved:

1. *Restraint:* There are three restraints which imply progressively curbing the activities of the body, mind and speech, i.e. aiming for single mindedness and avoiding what is not necessary.

2. *Watchfulness:* There are five types of Watchfulness involving positive caution in one's activities. These are (1) taking care when walking to avoid killing or hurting small creatures, (2) attempting to speak truthfully and as little as possible, (3) accepting alms in such a way that there is no feeling of self-gratification, (4) care in picking up and putting down objects so that no form of life is disturbed or crushed, and (5) care in performing the excretory functions so as not to disturb living things.

3. *Righteousness:* One cultivates ten rules of righteousness to reinforce these practices. These are perfection in forbearance, modesty, uprightness, truthfulness, purity, restraint, austerity (related to intense meditation), renunciation, detachment and continence.

4. *Reflections:* The twelve mental reflections engaged upon are given below.

The traditional approach makes them rather negative but Chitrabhanu (1981) has stated them in a more positive manner. Here, we integrate the two approaches. The twelve reflections are as follows:

(1) *Impermanence.* There is impermanence of everything surrounding one but there is unchanging soul beneath the changing body.

(2) *Helplessness.* We are helpless in the face of death but the inner invisible force always lives.

(3) *Cycle of Rebirth.* Liberation from the cycle of rebirth is possible.

(4) *Aloneness.* There is the absolute solitude of each individual as he goes through this cycle and therefore one should achieve dependence only on oneself.

(5) *Beyond Body.* The soul and body are separate and we are more than just corporeal. We must seek the true meaning of life through the existence of the soul.

(6) *Impurity.* How even the most physically attractive body contains impurity.

(7) *Karmic Fusion.* How karmic influx happens and how to stand apart and watch the inflow.

(8) *Karmic Shield.* How such influx may be stopped and how to close the window when the storm, in the form of the Four Passions, is about to come.

(9) *Total Karmic Decay.* How karmic matter within the soul may be shed so that the soul maybe cleaned to move towards permanent reality.

(10) *Universe.* The universe is eternal and uncreated, hence each person is responsible for his own salvation—for there is no God to intervene.

(11) *Rarity of True-Insight.* True-Insight is rarely attained and human embodiment bestows the rare privilege and opportunity to attain mokṣa.

(12) *Truth of Jain Path.* The truth of the teachings of the

Tirthankaras which leads to the goal of eternal peace through understanding one's own true nature.

5. *Afflictions' Mastery:* Mastery over afflictions consists of over twenty-two typical hardships which should be meditated upon; examples are hunger, thirst, cold, heat, insect bites and ridicule.

Table 8.1 gives a summary of various practices under different purification stages.

Note that the Three Restraints, the Five Watchfulnesses, the Ten Righteousnesses, etc. are only guidelines for laymen to give insight into possible procedures and they are not in general habitually carried out and even when they are, not always to perfection. The layman may carry out some of these (such as fasting on special days). However, the monk is expected at all times to follow these guidelines to near perfection. For instance, the diet of the monk is much more restricted than that of the layman.

Table 8.1 *Purification stages and the corresponding practices*

Purification Stage	Practices
1-4	Question: "Who am I?" Answer: "Belief in Axioms 1-3, 4A, 4B, 4C." [Practice Qualities (8) of True-Insight]
5	Layman's eleven renunciation sub-stages (see Fig. 8.1)
6	Restraints (3), Watchfulness (5), Righteousness (10), Reflections (12), Afflictions' Mastery (20).
7	Virtuous meditation.
8-10	First two pure trances.
12-14	Last two pure trances.

8.5 THE HIGHER STAGES AND MEDITATION

To move on to higher stages, one uses advanced meditation comprised of 'Virtuous Meditation' and 'Pure Trances'. These are part of the specific austerities under the Ten Righteousnesses, described in § 8.4. Virtuous Meditation entails deep contemplation[1] for upto 48 minutes on:

(i) the Jain teachings on nine reals;

(ii) the means by which to assist others;

(iii) karmic decay/emission; and
(iv) the structure of the universe.

(It is believed that on average one can maintain deep concentration for about 48 minutes.) During such periods, Carelessness is suppressed and the meditator temporarily attains the seventh stage. As he enters and leaves the contemplation periods, the meditator will be alternating between the sixth and seventh stages.

These contemplations, free from Carelessness, are considered to be preparatory to mokṣa but do not themselves lead to the defeat of the subtle passions. Only with the attainment of the eighth stage, "Unprecedented Spiritual Progress", can one be sure of reaching the highest step leading in the end to mokṣa. This can occur only through Pure Trances, of which there are four types:

(i) Pure Concentration on nature and multi-modal aspects of the six existents,
(ii) Pure Concentration on a unimodal aspect of an existent;
(iii) the transcendental state of subtle movement; and
(iv) the transcendental state of absolute immobility.

The first two Pure Trances operate in the eighth, ninth and tenth stages, during which both the subsidiary passions and very subtle passions are progressively suppressed or eliminated (see, § 7.4). Eventually the soul will gain sufficient energy to mount the ladder and so eliminate rather than suppress passion at each stage. Thus, the eleventh stage will be skipped and the soul will enter the twelfth stage. The purification of the soul is now at its highest which instantaneously moves to the thirteenth stage of "Dynamic Omniscience State".

Just a few moments before death, the last two Pure Trances are employed in succession and this sets the irreversible process of reaching the fourteenth stage. As mentioned in § 7.5, this stage lasts for at the most 48 minutes before physical death. Through the third Pure Trance, one completely stops the activities of the body, mind and speech except for the regulatory processes of breathing, heart-beat, etc. Through the fourth Pure Trance, even the regulatory processes are stopped, and the soul attains mokṣa.

We have concentrated on two positive meditations. There are also negative meditations or negative mental states. One is *Mournful Meditation* which is brooding on something disagreeable, e.g. the loss of loved ones or the loss of valued possessions. This mental state is a worry state. The other is *Wrathful Meditation* which is dwelling on the perpetration of violence, falsehood, theft, sexual deviations, and the extreme preservation of one's possessions. These states could exist upto the sixth purification stage. For further details on Jain-Yoga, we recommend Tatia (1986).

8.6 THE THREE JEWELS

Our axioms can be summarised into the following single verse of Umasvati,

"Right Faith, Right Knowledge and Right Conduct constitute the path to mokṣa"

(Appendix 3B, q. 8.2). Right Faith, Right Knowledge and Right Conduct are called the Three Jewels of the Jain path and these are attained sequentially; the Right Faith is the first to be achieved—this occurs at stage 4—then Right Conduct is achieved at stage 8 and Right Knowledge at stage 13, Fig. 8.2,

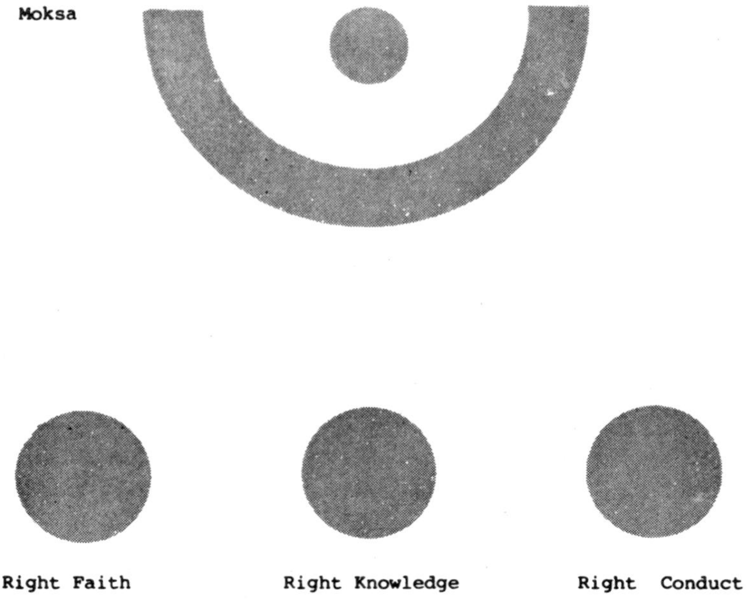

Fig. 8.2 The three 'jewels' of Jainism and mokṣa (swastika of Fig. 3.3 is depicted below these three jewels).

represents the traditional symbolic way of summarising these ideas (used normally in worship). They are usually depicted with the swastika beneath it to indicate the four directions of the mental states/four states of existence which have been given in Fig. 3.2. Of course, as described in § 7.2, "Right Faith (= True-Insight) consists of belief in the soul, karmic matter and the other seven Reals, the Right Knowledge is their comprehension and Right Conduct is austerity" (Appendix 3B, q. 8.3).

Right Knowledge also emphasises non-absolutism achieved through conditional predication, by thinking in relative terms through pluralism, scientific reasoning through the Jain syllogism, etc. (see, Ch. 9). It is said that the order of development is "first knowledge, then compassion" (Appendix 3B, q. 8.4). Right Conduct is austerity, already described in detail, but in fact blind austerities cannot take one very far. To quote, "if a man without Right Knowledge were to live on only a blade of grass once every month, he would not be entitled to even a sixteenth part of merit" (Appendix 3B, q. 8.5).

Note that, in practice, the effects of different levels of the Four Passions on an individual are as follows. With degree 4 of the Four Passions, neither one's faith nor conduct can be correct. With degree 3, one's faith is right but the renunciation of wrongful conduct is hindered. Degree 2 hinders complete self-discipline although Right Faith and partial self-discipline are achieved. Degree 1 allows complete self-discipline but there is some apathy in meditation and subtle attachment to the body. Degree 0 means that total self-discipline has been achieved.

Further, the karmic components are removed as follows. (We use the notation of § 5.4.) The karmic component (a_1) is removed at the fourth stage and (a_2) at the twelfth stage. The other three main components (b), (c) and (d) are removed at the thirteenth stage. All four secondary karmic components are removed simultaneously at the time of death in the fourteenth stage. It is worthwhile to note that in terms of Fig. 5.4, one starts by purifying the outer rectangles, leaving them blank and working towards the centre. When one has removed all the karmic matter, Fig. 5.4 is transformed to a single blank expanse with no boundaries, indicating pure soul.

One of the traditional analogies with the spiritual progress is the making of clarified butter (ghee) from milk. Table 8.2 shows the parallel, stage by stage. These stages are approximately identical to the order of the purification stages, as shown in the last column.

Table 8.2 *Analogy of purification stages with the stages in the production of clarified butter (ghee)*

Ghee Stages	Parallel	Purification Stage
1. From milk to make ghee	Realize existence of pure soul as Right Faith	4
↓	↓	
2. Heat milk	Do fasting (austerity)	5
↓	↓	
3. Cool milk	Cool mind (initial meditation)	6
↓	↓	
4. Add culture	Add Right Knowledge.	6
↓	↓	
5. Keep still for 6 hours	Take vow of silence (Right Conduct).	6
↓	↓	
6. Churn it to get butter	Advanced meditation.	7-11
↓	↓	
7. Then put it on the fire again to produce ghee	Fire=Advanced trances Ghee=Pure soul	12

8.7 ANALOGY OF THE SPIRITUAL PROGRESS WITH DRIVING A CAR

The spiritual progress of the individual through the fourteen stages can be illustrated by the process of learning to drive a car and then becoming increasingly skilled (Mardia, 1981). Note that the British test standard does not require perfection and that further improvement should take place after the test is passed. However, in life the individual is a "learner" until mokṣa is reached.

Stages 1 to 4 are equivalent to gaining a correct understanding of the use of the car—not that it is a vehicle to admire but a useful machine which must be driven in such a way that both oneself and others are not placed at risk. A person who believes, and can put into practice, this concept

Fig. 8.3 The Four Passions in a driver.

should be able to pass the British test. However, subsequent improvement may take place in order to become an advanced motorist, rather like the path of the monk.

Stages 5 and 6 involve the attainment of full restraint, that is, although in control of the car, one must nevertheless avoid accelerating quickly, braking hard, or flashing lights/hooting unnecessarily. Fig. 8.3. shows the manifestation of the Four Passions in a driver. The Three Restraints mean a progressive curbing of the activities of the body, mind and speech so that one acts instinctively, without conscious thought. Stage 7 is the achievement of Watchfulness, i.e. using mirrors, indicators, lights, etc. when necessary so that no other user is made anxious by one's bad driving, even though an accident would have been unlikely. Also, one is alert at every moment so that enough time is allowed to take corrective action on the bad driving of others, etc. Stages 8 to 12 involve the reduction and elimination of passions in driving. These are the most difficult faults to remove and involve feelings such as impatience in a long traffic jam, and uneasiness when being repeatedly overtaken, even though driving at just below the maximum legal speed. These passions may smoulder and only arise occasionally, since they are usually kept in check. At stage 13, one has reached the position of causing the minimum possible danger on the road. Stage 14 is the beginning of the cessation of activity which means that one sees that doing without a car altogether eliminates this contribution to danger. Note that none of these activities takes place whilst the car is stationary with the engine not running, i.e. there is no yoga. It should be remembered that this is a less than perfect analogy.

We can also illustrate the use of the Five Watchfulnesses through this same analogy. The first Watchfulness is rather like driving so as not to hit birds, rabbits, etc. on the road. The second is similar to reducing conversation in the car to decrease distractions. The third can be likened to not drinking and driving, thereby retaining full-concentration. The fourth is like looking around the car before starting and choosing a parking space carefully so that no child or animal is hit. The last Watchfulness is the avoidance of running the car engine in a confined space where people may be affected by the exhaust fumes.

8.8 GLOSSARY

1. *Eight qualities of the True-Insight* (= Aṣṭāṅga)
   Freedom from doubt=Niḥśaṁkita
   Freedom from anticipation=Niḥkāṃkṣita
   Freedom from disgust=Nirvicikitsā
   Freedom from false notions=Amūḍhadṛṣṭi
   Safeguarding=Upagūhana
   Promoting stability=Sthitīkaraṇa
   Illumination=Prabhāvanā
   Disinterested love=Vātsalya
2. *Five Lower Vows (= Aṇuvrata) of Jain Layman* (= Śrāvaka)
   Non-violence=Ahiṃsā
   Truthfulness=Satya
   No-stealing=Asteya
   No sexual deviations=Anu Brahmavrata
   Non-possession=Aparigraha
   (Model steps of renunciation = Pratimā)
3. *Anitidotes to Karmic Forces*
   Restraint = Gupti [three: mana (mind), vachan (speech) and kāyā (body)]
   Watchfulness=Samiti
   Righteousness=Dharma
   Ten-fold Righteousness=Daśa-Dharma
   Reflections=Anupreksa: [Anitya, Asaraṣa, Mokṣa, Ekatva, Anyatva, Asucya, Āsrava, Samvara, Nirjarā, Loka-ākāśa, Bodhi-durlabha, Dharma-svākhyātatva]
   Afflictions mastery=Parīsahajaya
   Right Conduct=Samayak-cāritra
4. Meditation=*Dhyānas*
   (1) Mournful Meditation=Ārtadhyāna
   (2) Wrathful Meditation=Rutradhyāna
   (3) Virtuous Meditation=Dharmadhyāna
   (4) Pure Trance=Śukladhyānā
5. *Three Jewels (=tri-ratna)*
   Right Faith=Samyak-darśana
   Right Knowledge=Samyak-jñāna
   Right Conduct=Samyak-cāritra

NOTES

1. P.S. Jaini, pp. 252-3. "Dharmadhyāna entails the intense contemplation, for a short period (up to fortyeight minutes), of one of several objects: (1) the teachings of the Jina on the nine tattvas and how these teachings can best be communicated to others (*ājñāvicaya*); (2) the great misery suffered by other beings (whose minds are impelled by passions and blinded by ignorance) and the means by which these beings can be saved (*apāyavicaya*); (3) the mysterious mechanisms of karmic influx, binding, duration, and outcome and the fact that the soul is fundamentally independent of these processes and thus able to disengage itself therefrom (*vipākavicaya*); (4) the structure of the universe and the interplay of causes that brings souls to their particular destinies *(samsthānavicaya)*."

9

JAIN LOGIC

9.1 INTRODUCTION

THE JAIN BELIEF is that the purer the soul, the higher is its knowledge, perception, bliss and energy. Only omniscience can perceive the entire truth of reality or the nine reals. However, we are left with the other four types of knowledge, namely through mind and senses, scriptures (the highest authority in the field!), clairvoyance and mind-reading. As in science, one either accepts the assertions as theories established by the authorities in the field (which we mostly do), or one verifies every assertion for oneself (which we are rarely able to do). However, there should be some plausible principles which one can adopt for any enquiry undertaken. Further, there is always room for some improvement. We give details of a few main principles of Jain logic which allow conclusions to be drawn when the types of questions asked do not lead to complete certainty or complete uncertainty. Note that the present theories in Particle Physics (see, Ch. 10) rely heavily on such a principle.

The Jains have developed a remarkable theory of knowledge and its acquisition. It is a complex topic but we give a brief sketch (Tattvartha-sutra, tr. Tatia, Chps. 1, 5; 1994). Broadly speaking, this topic has three major components:

1. Pramana (organs of knowledge/ the approved means of knowledge);
2. Naya (standpoints/philosophical standpoints);
3. Anekantavada (holistic principle).
   of which Sydavada (conditional predication) forms an essential part.

Knowledge about an object is obtained through two processes—(i) a partial process; and (ii) a total process. The total process is termed Pramana (organs of knowledge). This method not only gives credence to observational processes but also to the process of mental faculty. Because of the involvement of both these faculties, it gives a total view of an object. The partial process is called Naya (standpoint). This involves the study of an object with respect to one single aspect at a time. There may be many aspects and so there could be many standpoints. This, however, does not give a complete picture of the object.

There are two types of organs of knowledge (i) direct and (ii) indirect. The direct has two varieties: sensory and supersensory. Sensory knowledge consists of processes of recollection, recognition, concomitance and inference. Note that the syllogism given below is a part of inference. Jain theory postulates clairvoyance, mind-reading and omniscience as supersensory direct knowledge. The main scriptures form the prime source of indirect knowledge. Any direct knowledge expressed verbally is called an indirect source of knowledge. For classifications of such knowledge, see Tattvartha-sutra, (Tr. Tatia, 1994, p. 15).

The standpoints serve as a base for the gradual and complete comprehension about an object. This can be in two ways: one the basis of the properties of the object and another on the basis of verbal expressions about them. They start from an overall picture of the object to its final picture, in its properties as well as in its verbal expressions. On this basis, there are seven types of standpoints postulated in Jainism:

The common person's view, generic view, practical view, linear view, lieral view, etymological view and actuality view. These can be interpreted with respect to time. The first represents all the three tenses whereas the linear view represents the current moment and the actuality view represents only the present tense and the current moment. Thus, knowledge moves from grosser to finer quality with respect to particular aspects of these standpoints.

We now describe a few specific Jain doctrines of logic.

9.2 SYLLOGISM

We will first consider the Jain syllogism. A 'medium' syllogism of Jain consists of five propositions. For example,

1. Tom died, Dick died and so did Harry.

2. Tom, Dick and Harry are truly universal types of men.
3. Therefore, all men die.
4. John is a man.
5. Therefore, John will die.

The last three terms of the medium syllogism can, of course, be recognised as the Aristotelian syllogism which would be:

Man is mortal.
John is a man.
Therefore, John is mortal.

The medium syllogism clearly combines inductive and deductive methods of reasoning. In fact, it reflects the main stages of scientific/statistical thinking. The first two terms can be thought of as taking observations from a population and the third term as drawing inference from the observations. The last two terms give a projection about a new observation. This empirical logic is the basis of scientific methods and should not be lost sight of in all scientific applications.

In fact, the syllogism is said to be accurate when its all five parts are in harmony with each other. For the example above, the five parts are:

(1) John will die, (2) because he is a man,
(3) like Tom, Dick and Harry, (4) as they died,
(5) therefore he will die.

A syllogism is said to constitute a fallacy (ābhāsa) if any of these five parts are discordant with our observations.

9.3 THE CONDITIONAL PREDICATION PRINCIPLE

Another central feature of this system is a principle of conditional predications (called Syadvada) in which one examines inference from seven standpoints (Saptabhangi-naya) prefixed by "maybe":

(1) it is (from one standpoint);
(2) it is not;
(3) it is and is not;
(4) it is indeterminate;
(5) it is and is indeterminate;
(6) it is not and is indeterminate;
(7) it is, is not and is indeterminate.

Note that all predications have a margin of uncertainty, and each of the seven predictions may be called a Naya as it represents one aspect of an object. Predication (1) can be visualised as 'green' at a set of traffic lights, (2) as 'red'. Its special feature is (4) which allows the possibility of indeterminacy, i.e. 'amber'. Other predications are syntheses of (1) and (2) with (4). "Maybe" is not a good translation of the word "syat"; another translation is "from one standpoint".

+ = Maybe **IT IS** (from one standpoint)
– = Maybe it is not
$\pm$ = Maybe **IT IS** and it is not
? = Maybe *IT IS INDETERMINATE*
+? = Maybe **IT IS** and is also *INDETERMINATE*
–? = Maybe it is not and is also *INDETERMINATE*
$\pm$? = Maybe **IT IS** and it is not and is also *INDETERMINATE*

Fig. 9.1 Schematic representation of the seven conditional predications: + = Bold capital letters, – = Capital letters, ? = Italic capital letters.

Thus, we can come to qualitative judgement. A schematic picture is given in Fig. 9.1. We know that in every act of observation, the observer is involved. The above principle attempts perception without the observer, but allowing for the margin of error.

Kothari (1975) has pointed out that the superposition principle of quantum mechanics provides an illuminating example of Syadvada. Let Kets (a) $|\alpha'>$ and (b) $|\alpha''>$ be the different eigenstates of an observable α for a quantum mechanical system. Let an inexpressible state be represented by (c) $|P> = |\alpha'> + |\alpha''>$. Then in the terminology of Fig. 9.1, we identify the above quantities as follows:

(a) by +, (b) by –, and (c) by = ?.

Bharucha (1993) has provided "truth tables" of Syadvada and Quantum logic.

9.4 THE CONDITIONAL HOLISTIC PRINCIPLE

We have described methods of looking at sub-parts of the problem through conditional predication. However, the knowledge is to be combined through, for example, the repeated use of the syllogism. Consider first the following example. There are six blind men who want to know what kind of object an elephant is. Each touches a different part of the

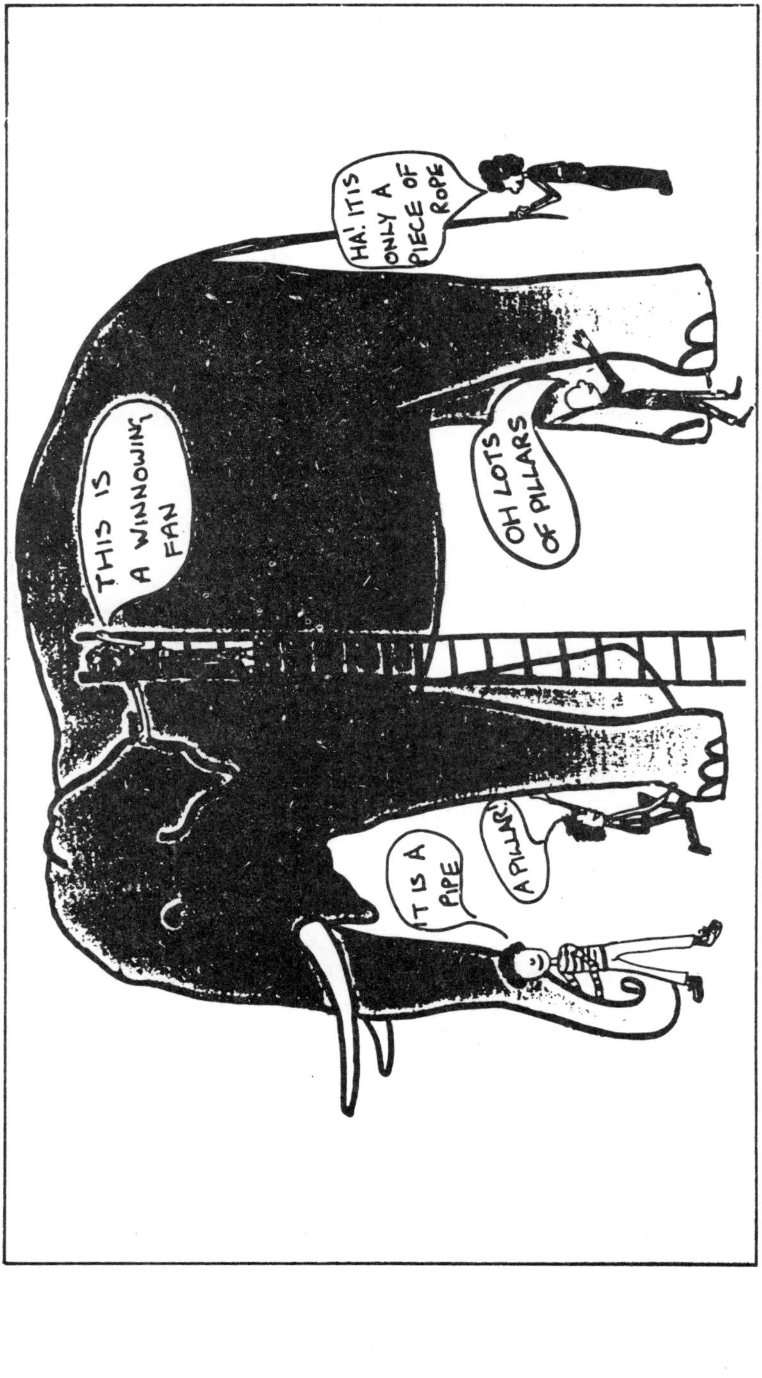

Fig. 9.2 A depiction of Jain Holistic Principle: Elephant and six blind men (five shown).

elephant (see, Fig. 9.2). The one who touches a leg says "It is a pillar", the one who touches the trunk says " It is a pipe", the one who touches an ear says "This is a winnowing fan", and so on. Thus, each opinion differs. Hence, if we wish to understand what kind of object the elephant is, we must look at it from all sides. In the context of this elephant illustration, Pramana is involved in its "direct" section of sensory observation, namely, the use of touch. Each blindman forms an example under the category of Naya. (The story seems to be popularized first in the West in a poem by J.G. Saxe (1816-1877); Mardia (1991) quotes this poem in full.)

This illustrates the Jain Holistic Principle (Anekantavada). We now apply it to a real example. Consider the following conditional predicates:

(1) Earth may be round.
(2) Earth may not be round.
(3) Earth may, or may not, be round.
(4) Earth may be of indeterminate shape.
(5) Earth may be round or may be of indeterminate shape.
(6) Earth may not be round or may be of indeterminate shape.
(7) Earth may or may not be round, or may be of indeterminate shape.

We reach the conclusion that the Earth is round from a global standpoint but is not round from a local standpoint. A similar conclusion may be reached about Mars and Venus. Therefore, the same may be true for all the planets.

Applying the syllogism to a new planet which has these same properties, we may conclude that this planet is round from a global standpoint but is not round from a local standpoint.

Thus we come to the Conditional (non-absolute) Holistic Principle. The Conditional Predications applied to each entity are beads which are held together by the Holistic Principle behaving like a thread.

9.5 DISCUSSIONS

Here we have discussed only a small fraction of Jain logic and philosophy. Note that the holistic (manifold) aspect is the key to the system and is usually applied to ontological questions. Each existent is composed of three aspects: substance, quality and mode. Also, for each unilateral aspect, four factors are important to each situation; the specific "object", its specific location, its specific time and its specific state. The Holistic Principle attempts to view the existents from these multi-modal aspects. In practice this principle implies that one should avoid extreme views and also take a broad view rather than a narrow one.

Matilal (1981) has argued that the Holistic Principle provides a philosophy of synthesis. Its essence lies in exposing and making explicit the standpoints or assumptions of different philosophical schools. As a philosophical methodology it takes its flight on the two wings: the standpoint principle and the conditional predication principle.

For a quantitative study inspired by the Conditional Predication Principle, we refer to Haldane (1957) where it is seen how we can apply the system to learning experiments, such as that of Pavlov. Mardia (1975, 1988a) indicates some other aspects including the relationship of Jain logic with Karl Popper (1968), who claims that we cannot have absolutely true scientific laws. For a comprehensive treatment we refer to Tatia (1984); for Jain syllogism see J.L. Jaini (1916). We conclude with the following quotation from Mahalanobis (1954) on Jain views:

> "Finally, I should draw attention to the realist and pluralist views of Jain philosophy and the continuing emphasis on the multiform and infinitely diversified aspects of reality which amounts to the acceptance of an "open" view of the universe with scope for unending change and discovery."

9.6 GLOSSARY

Jain Holistic Principle = Anekāntavāda
Conditional Predication Principle = Syādvāda
Standpoint principle = Nayavāda
Organs of Knowledge/Comprehensive Right Knowledge = Pramāṇa
Classification of imports of words = Nikṣepa
The seven-fold conditional predication = Saptabhaṅgi-naya
maybe it is (from one standpoint) = syādasti
maybe it is not = syātnāsti

maybe it is and is not = syādasti nāsti ca
maybe it is indeterminate = syādavaktavyah
maybe it is and is indeterminate = syādasti ca avaktavyaśca
maybe it is not and is
  indeterminate = syātnāsti ca avaktavyaśca
maybe it is, is not and is
  indeterminate = syādasti nāsti ca avaktavyaśca
(Maybe = syāt, indeterminate = avaktavya)

Knowledge = jñāna
Matijñāna = empirical knowledge
Śrutajñāna = verbal/articulate knowledge
Avadhijñāna = clairvoyance
Manahparyayajñāna = mind reading
Kevalajñāna = infinite/omniscience knowledge

10
JAINISM AND MODERN SCIENCE

10.1 ANALOGIES

TO CALL JAINISM simply a religion is a misrepresentation since it tries to give a unified scientific basis for the whole cosmos including "living and non-living" entities. Thus, it is a Holistic science which encompasses everything including religion. The main contributions of science in this era and their parallels with Jainism are as follows (Mardia, 1988b). In the discussion below, one should bear in mind that Jain Science is very much qualitative. However, Jain Science goes beyond Modern Science in many places, but only rarely do the two conflict.

(1) *Particle physics and quantum theory.* It is only in this century that technology has advanced to the point where atomic processes and elementary particles may be studied and understood in detail. However, it is interesting to note that Jains had formulated their ideas presumably one step further by evolving the concept of karmons. Whether such particles exist or not may be debatable, but it is interesting that they fit in well with a self-regulatory universe and the life in it.

Quantum theory is very much probabilistic. In some cases it is very near the probabilistic Jain Principle of Conditional Predication (see, Ch. 9). This principle is partly a probabilistic principle connected with the reductionistic principle of science. Jain would complement this principle with the Holistic Principle (see, Ch. 9). At present, science is moving within these two principles. However, there are claims that the world is made up of objects whose existence is independent of soul (human consciousness): this turns out to be in conflict with quantum theory and with facts established by experiment (see, d'Espagnat, 1979). There are also attempts to bring the consciousness components into quantum theory models (see,

Jahn, 1982). As a first introduction to the subject of quantum theory and reality, we refer the reader to Gamow (1965) and Gribbin (1984).

(2) *Evolution.* One of the greatest achievements of the biological science of the last century has been Darwin's theory of evolution. It is interesting to note that through the density of karmic matter in living species, one goes beyond evolution and tries to encompass the whole of creation. It tries to answer the fundamental question of the evolution of life as an individual mechanism.

(3) *Exchangeability of matter and energy.* One of the most revolutionary ideas of Albert Einstein was the claim that matter can be converted to energy and vice versa, i.e. matter and energy are exchangeable. This concept has been with Jains for centuries. *Pudgala* is the word that is used to describe this phenomenon (see, Ch. 4). Explicit in this word is that matter and energy are the two sides of the same coin. As we know there is no terminology to describe this phenomenon in the Greek language and therefore no such scientific expression. The best one can do is to write mass-energy for this profound concept.

(4) *Fundamental forces.* Science recognises at present four fundamental forces:

gravitational, electro-magnetic, weak nuclear and strong nuclear. Investigations are in progress to reduce these forces to a single "superforce". Importantly, Jain's concept of karmic force/ animation force, which must be an additional force requiring further studies, might explain various non-physical phenomena such as mind over matter. If such forces do exist, the underlying particles of this force are karmons which have subtle properties because of their absorption into anything living. Thus it will make tracking them down much more difficult.

In Ch. 4, we have mentioned that the two Jain existents—Dynamic and Stationary Media—can be viewed as Dynamic and Stationary forces which allow interaction (non-uniform motion) and equilibrium (in uniform motion?) between/ within soul and matter. This may be the qualitative answer to a super-force. Jain, G.R. (1975) identifies the Dynamic Medium as the non-material Aether of space, whereas the Stationary

Medium is identified as the unified force of Gravitation and Electro-magnetism.

We now discuss these in detail in the following sections.

10.2 MODERN PARTICLE PHYSICS

As is already known, the discovery of electrons at the end of the last century by J.J. Thomson led to further investigation of similar constituents of chemical elements, namely atoms. It was around 1910 that Rutherford and others first discovered that atoms contain electrons and a nucleus. (The nucleus contains neutrons and protons which are collectively called nucleons.) It is known that electrons are negatively charged particles (charge = –1) and neutrons are uncharged particles, that is, electrically neutral. The simplest example of the atomic structure of a chemical element is provided by hydrogen, which has one electron and one proton; however, its 'isotopes' can have either one or two neutrons without disturbing its chemical properties. For chemical stability, the number of electrons is always equal to the number of protons.

In the early 1970's, the picture changed completely (see, Fig. 10.1). There are now three groups of elementary particles:

Quarks, Leptons and Gauge Bosons.

The bosons form a glue between the other two.Quarks differ from leptons in that quarks have fractional charges, namely 2/3, 1/3, – 1/3, and –2/3, whereas leptons have charge O or –1. Further, bosons differ from the other two because quarks and leptons have 1/2-spin, whereas bosons have 1-spin. The electron is an example of a lepton with charge-1. The neutrino is an example of a lepton with no charge.

Quarks can exist in clusters of two or three. One can have three quarks as in the proton. The groups containing three quarks are called "baryons", and the groups containing only two quarks under certain compatability conditions are called "mesons". In the latter case, there can be one quark with one anti-quark. The simplest example of a meson is the "positive pion" which consists of one quark with one anti-quark. Note that like electrons, quarks are assessed to be perfect points without any structure.

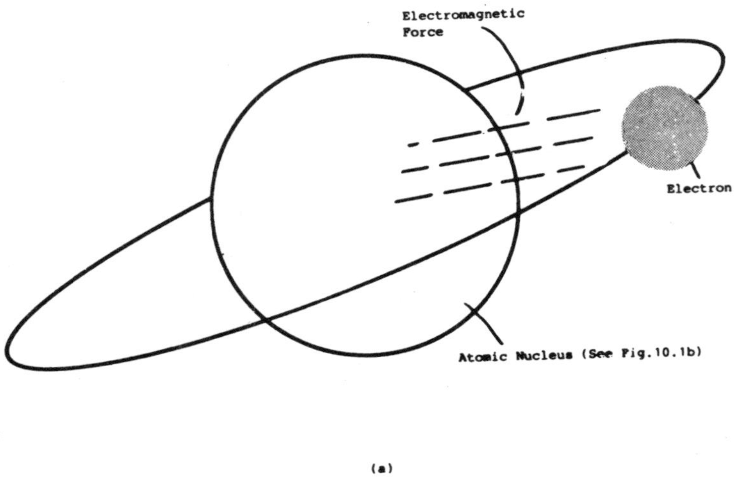

Fig. 10.1 (a) Hydrogen atom with a single electron, atomic nucleus and the strong nuclear force.

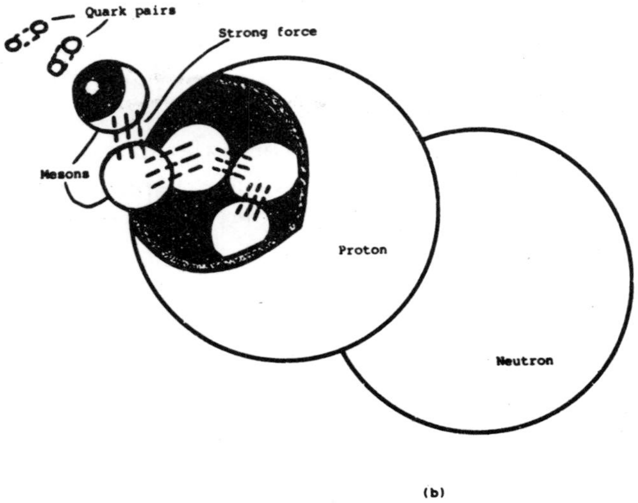

Fig. 10.1 (b) Sub-atomic particles of the hydrogen atom: neutron, proton with its mesons and quarks.

The following are the properties which distinguish various elementary particles:

(1) Charge or no charge (colour).
(2) Mass.
(3) Spin (intrinsic angular momentum).
(4) Lifespan.
(5) Force (four types, see § 10.3).

Note that baryons have the greatest mass and leptons have the smallest mass, with bosons having an intermediate mass. Quarks have six flavours and three colours. Note that the use of these flavours and colours is only symbolic. Amongst the so-called six flavours, the most important are "up" and "down" (for the lightest pair of quarks). If "u" denotes up-quark and "d" denotes down-quark, then the corresponding notations for an anti-particle are "ū" and "d" respectively. A positive pion is then either ud or ūd. The three colours are red, green and blue: these are the three "electrical" colours.

10.3 FOUR FORCES IN NATURE

The four fundamental forces in Nature are gravitational, electromagnetic, weak nuclear and strong nuclear. These are all thought to operate through gauge bosons. The particles interact via a gauge boson as a heavy snowball exchanged between two skaters; e.g. for two electrons (the skaters), the photon (the snowball) tells one electron of the presence of the other electron and then induces a response: this is the electro-magnetic force (see, Fig. 10.2a). In the case of the two

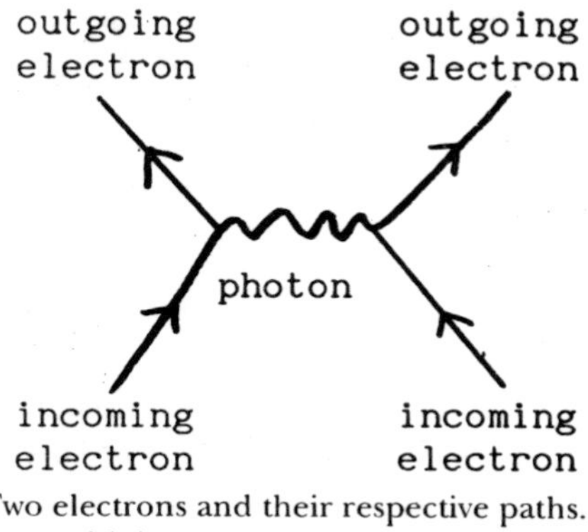

Fig. 10.2 (a) Two electrons and their respective paths. Electro-magnetic force with its gauge boson 'photon' (zig-zag line).

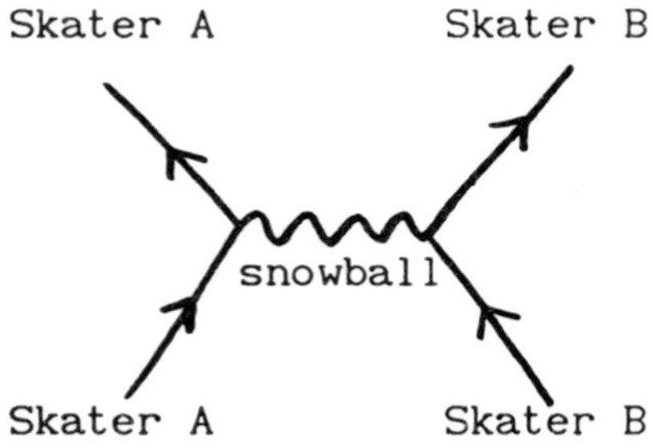

Fig. 10.2 (b) Two skaters exchanging a snowball.

skaters, say A and B (Fig. 10.2b), skater A throws (emits) the snowball (photon) on skater B, who will be recoiled (the weak-force), after which the snowball disintegrates (is absorbed). These are Feynman diagrams.

Recall that the force acting between a proton and a neutron in the nucleus is a strong nuclear force (see, Fig. 10.1). The, strong nuclear force acts between the baryons through a coloured gluon (see, Fig. 10.3). Baryons feel the

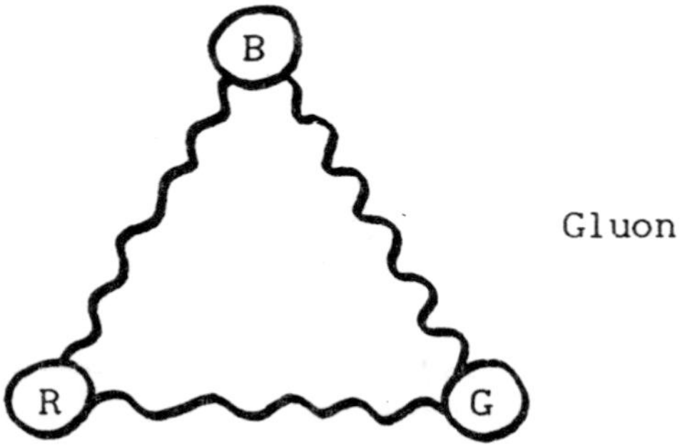

Fig. 10.3 A baryon with its quarks (in circles, red—R, green—G, blue—B) and the strong nuclear force with its gauge boson 'gluon' (zig-zag lines).

strong force, whereas leptons do not feel this froce since they do not have a colour. The energetic quarks radiate gluon; however, as they emerge, the gluons must neutralise their colour which they do by converting the energies through observable particles, mainly mesons. The weak nuclear force underlies radioactivity: the particles Z and (W^+, W^-) are the

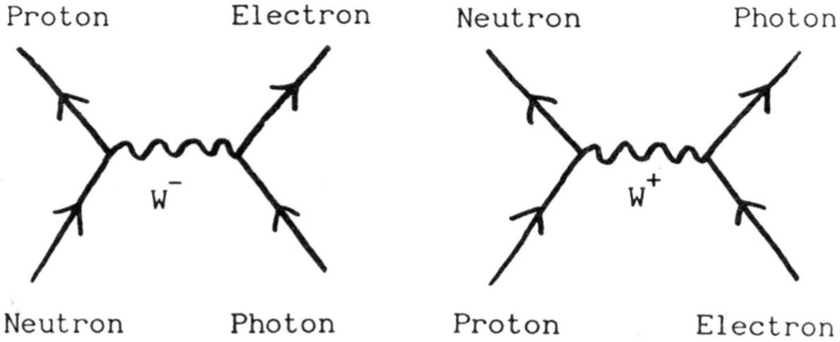

Fig. 10.4 Weak force: (a) a neutron and a photon exchanging W^+ and (b) a proton and an electron exchanging W.

gauge bosons of the weak nuclear force for the electrically charged and neutral versions, respectively (see, Fig. 10.4). The gravitational force (see, Fig. 10.5), which is the weakest of the four, holds matter together in the bulk, but the evidence for a particle to transmit gravity—the graviton—is very limited.

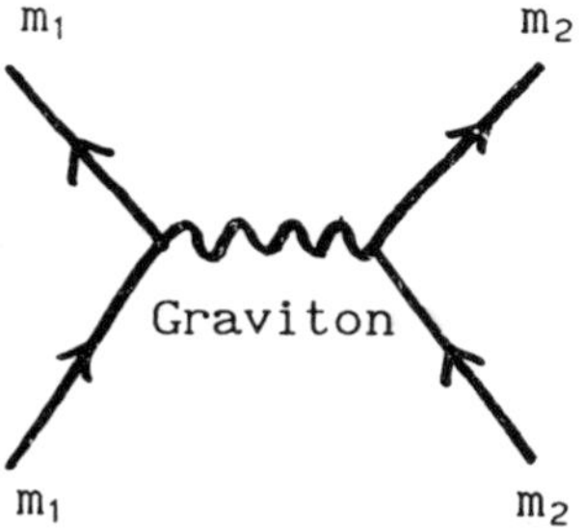

Fig. 10.5 Gravitational force between two mesons (m_1, m_2) and gravitons.

We could add karmic forces to the list. Karmic fields are also non-material regions of influence extending in space and continuing in time, but allow interaction between the non-living and the living, i.e. soul and karmons. For karmic forces, it seems that the bosons for interaction between the soul and karmons are 'Passions' (a form of karmic radiation), except that under no-Passion (a force-shield) there can only be karmic radiation (see, Fig. 10.6) but no karmic fusion. Perhaps we could term these two bosons as 'Passiono' and 'Apassiono' particles, respectively. At another level, (see, S.K. Jain, 1980) luminous force might explain the cycles of rebirth in the form of energy (luminous capsule) released as electro-magnetic type of waves at the time of death. Thus it can travel instantaneously at a long distance carrying specific messages, e.g. in karmic body. For example, the karmic body might carry pheromones (the chemical components produced by an animal carrying individualized communication) etc. in the karmic body which are attached and transfused with the zygote (the zygote is the first cell resulting from the union of two parental germ cells of the new born). The "energy" received by the zygote could induce predestined changes in DNA (the genetic code of life). However, a deeper study of this topic is required.

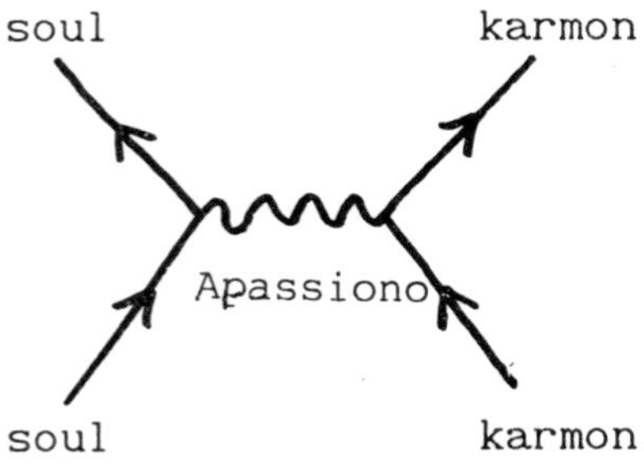

Fig. 10.6 Karmic force with an apassiono' as its boson.

10.4 SOME FURTHER ANALOGIES

Various similarities between Modern and Jain Particle physics have already been pointed out by Jain, G.R. (1975) and Zaveri (1975).

The five attributes of Jain ultimate particles given in § 4.5 might be equated to present Physics as follows, but, of course, this is somewhat arbitrary.

(i) Five colours = 3 charge colours of quarks+ two charges of positive and negative as white and black.

(ii) Five flavours = flavours of quarks and leptons. (The sixth flavour of quarks is not yet established.)

(iii) Two smells = spin of 1 and ½.

(iv) Touch: (a) Palpability = Gauge bosons. (G.R. Jain identifies it with positive and negative charges.)

(b) Temperature = Radiation.

Intensity of palpability = Energy levels.

(The rule of combining the ultimate particles given in § 4.5 is similar to Pauli's exclusion principle.)

(v) Two kinds of ultimate particles: effect (action) and cause particles = particle and its anti-particle. (G.R. Jain identifies these with the electron and the positron, respectively.)

Some other comments are as follows. In some sense the ultimate particles are particles and in another sense they are energies. The properties of ultimate particles related to motion and state are probabilistic and seem to reflect Heisenberg's uncertainty principle. Further, the ultimate particle cannot be obstructed or stopped in motion except when in an aggregate. Thus, it is like a neutrino, or maybe like a Tachyon, of speed greater than that of a photon.

In addition to the four fields corresponding to the four established forces in Nature, Sheldrake (1981) puts forward a "morphic field" corresponding to "morphic resonance"; Jain Science relies on a "karmic field". Time and space are the usual four dimensions but a fifth dimension of mass is regarded as essential in some new relativity theories: note that the definition of a "space point/spatial unit" of Jains is regarded as a point with dimensions (however infinitesimally small) and all the ultimate particles in the universe can be contained in this single point (see, Basham, 1953, pp. 77-78). Thus the Big-Bang theory is alluded to. Also, Basham (1953, p. 78) quotes an old Jain verse—"The complex of dimensional points is horizontal, while that of which the function is characterized by moments (time) is vertical." Thus time is the fourth dimension.

One of the present leading pioneers in modern physics is Stephen Hawking. He argues that the universe has no beginning and no end (see, Hawking, 1988, p. 116) and this idea clearly underlies the Jain universal cycles described in § 6.4. Again, his claim that the universe is finite is implicit in the Jain concept of the universe. The concept of the black hole (Hawking, 1988) has some similarity to Mokṣa as pointed out in § 4.4. The boundary between occupied and unoccupied space is also similar to 'event horizon' which stands for the boundary of the black hole (see, Hawking, 1988, p. 89). However, one would prefer to reach Mokṣa rather than a black hole! The claim that thoughts are made of particles is also in accord with Jain science.

10.5 CONCLUDING REMARKS

Modern science is in a state of fermentation and entirely new concepts of matter and of fields are appearing. Readers interested further in an overview of Science and 'Religion' are recommended to Davies (1983) and Khursheed (1987). We conclude with a few of Einstein's views (Einstein, 1940, 1941). First, his concept of religion is very near that of Jains:—

"......a person who is religiously enlightened appears to me to be one who has, to the best of his ability, liberated himself from the fetters of his selfish desires......"

Secondly, his attitude (Einstein, 1940, 1941) to Science and Religion is worth bearing in mind:

"......there also belongs the faith in the possibility that the regulations valid for the world of existence are rational, that is, comprehensible to reason. I cannot conceive of a genuine scientist without that profound faith. The situation may be expressed by an image:

Science without religion is lame,
Religion without science is blind."

EPILOGUE

SINCE THE FIRST EDITION, the author has had the privilege of giving general seminars at various centres based on the book. These lectures gave an opportunity to adapt the main ideas as a basis for a single seminar presentation. We give below an abstract (Mardia, 1991) which would be particularly useful for the younger generation. The recent works by Singhvi, L.M. (1991), Shah, A.(1990) and Tobias (1991) are also highly recommended.

1. KARMONS AND THE KARMIC PERSONAL COMPUTER

Einstein said that

> Religion without science is blind,
> Science without religion is lame.

Jainism is science with religion. Every aspect of Jainism is based on understanding the cosmos, and the living and non-living entities in it. Modern science is capable of illuminating part of the truth. It explains matter in terms of forces and small particles. Electricity, through electrons, gives rise to light in the room; radio-waves through electric-magnetic forces, result in sound on a loudspeaker and so on. Jainism explains life through the interaction of such invisible small particles and the soul. The small particles are *Karmic Particles* or *Karmons* and they create a *Karmic Force.* We keep on absorbing these karmons through activity, and throw some out after their effect has taken place. Thus the soul has a *Karmic Computer* attached to it. This personal karmic computer keeps all the records—it also dictates some tasks from previous records, i.e. past lives. For example, your karmic computer has in it a message for you to read this book—to think about the Jain religion. This is a good activity and therefore the soul absorbs positive karmons. These positive karmons lead to positive fruition. Also positive action reduces negative karmons and the soul gets purified. Thus the Karmic matter and the soul form a type of nuclear reactor, say, *Karmic Reactor* and the purification is like the emission of powerful energy from this karmic reactor.

Jainism uses words like *Bandha* (karmic fusion), *Āsrava* (karmic force-lines), etc. to describe these activities. Just as the basis of modern physics is its forces, Jainism is based on karmic force. As modern science believes in the interchangeability of matter and energy, in the same way the reaction between karmic matter and soul takes place. Jains have used the word *Pudgala* (*pud* = join, *gala* = break) for this mass-energy equivalence. There is no such word for this concept in modern science because the terminology of modern science is derived from Greek/Latin.

2. KARMIC FUSION AND VEGETARIANISM

Our aim is to minimize the intake of these karmons. That is one of the reasons why vegetarianism has become part of Jainism. True Jains will not eat onions etc. but will eat apples etc. You might wonder the reason for this? The reason put forward is that there are more *life units* in an onion than in an apple. From one apple tree, one gets a large number of apples but from one onion one gets only another onion. Thus an onion must have more life units than that of an apple! Therefore the consumption of onions gives rise to the intake of more karmons than apples. You can extend this idea to other foods—thus Jains operate a very strict type of vegetarianism, consuming neither meat, fish or eggs. They confine themselves to grains, vegetables and milk products.

3. KARMONS AND OBSCURATION OF KNOWLEDGE

To bring rationality into thinking one should also examine at Jain Logic. Jainism believes in the principle of conditional predication (*Syādvāda*) so that everything is conditioned by our knowledge at a particular time—and there is nothing absolutely known unless the soul is "perfect"— that is, when the divine quality of *Jainness* is fully developed. Soul with karmic matter is like crude oil compared with petrol; the more refined it is the more power it has. Non-absolutism in thinking is what is recommended in Jainism. This principle operates clearly in the scientific research; yesterday the smallest particle was the proton—today it is a quark and so on.

Also Jain logic recommends relativity in thinking on the holistic principle called *Anekāntavāda*. Consider the example of the six blind men and an elephant. One who touches the tail says it is a rope, one who touches the leg says it is a pillar and so on. What one requires is to look at every aspect of life and matter. This story was popularized in the West in a poem by J.G. Saxe (1816-77).

4. THE PURIFICATION PATH

In short, according to Jainism, time, space, life, non-life (matter) exist and will exist forever—the universe is self-regulating; life is mainly regulated by karmons unless these are all removed. How can these be removed? A path of purification is prescribed. It is not easy since Jainism believes existing karmic matter can only be removed (before predetermined duration) through austerity, otherwise the personal karmic computer will keep on working. It prescribes self-restraint rather than self-indulgence. Einstein when he tried to define his concept of religion, said

> "......a person who is religiously enlightened appears to me to be one who has to the best of his ability, liberated himself from the fetters of his selfish desires."

This is, indeed, a definition of Jainism!

5. SELF-RESTRAINT AND THE ENVIRONMENTAL ISSUES

The purification prescription includes the endeavour to live a life of moderation and to practise a measure of abstinence and austerity so that one does not overburden the universe and its resources. The Jain's principle of non-violence covers not only loving oneself but compassion towards all animals and human beings. Even domestic animals may not be roped or whipped except occasionally and then always mercifully with due consideration and without anger. Obsession and clinging to possessions, and enjoyment for personal ends should be minimized always with charity in the forefront. Obsessive attachment to possessions and collecting objects of desire is a psychedelic state — a state of trance. (*Mūrchā parigrahaḥ*,

Tattvartha sutra, Ch. 7, verse 17). In general, the attitude of managing personal wealth as trustees for social benefit is recommended i.e. the idea of non-personal possession is invoked. Total awareness is important at all times. Just as "one minute of negative thoughts" could create havoc in an undisciplined life through heavy karmons: "one minute of positive thoughts" would gain for a long-term peace and harmony in a disciplined life through light karmons (cf. Tobias, 1991, p. 90).

The emphasis on preservation of the environment is emphasised by the colour coding (leśyā = stain) of the karmic density of soul. There are six consecutive levels: black, blue, grey, yellow, lotus-pink and luminous white. The first three represent heavier karmic density whereas the next three represent lighter karmic density. J.L. Jaini (1916) connects these with the colours of the human aura. In practice, an analogy of picking fruits from a tree is used to classify the degree of colur stain. A person with the first level uproots the tree for its fruits, the second cuts the tree from its trunk, the third cuts a branch, the fourth cuts off a bunch, the fifth plucks ripe fruit from the tree and the sixth merely picks up ripe fruit fallen to the ground. Thus the person with the highest spiritual level has the total preservation of the environment in the forefront. Furthermore, the karmon intake is increased on creating waste and pollution since these are regarded as acts of violence (cf. Singhvi, 1990). The cue is taken from "the bee that sucks honey in the blossoms of a tree without hurting the blossom meanwhile strengthening itself."

APPENDICES

APPENDIX 1: THE LIFE OF MAHAVIRA

MAHAVIRA WAS BORN in 599 B.C. in Kundagrama, then a large city in Northern India near the modern city of Patna. His father was King Siddhārtha and his mother Triśalā. His original name, Vardhamāna, which means "ever growing" was given to him because everything in the kingdom became abundant during the period of his mother's pregnancy.

He soon developed a great sense of understanding and rapport with animals. Even in his childhood he courageously subdued a terrifying snake. He also calmed an elephant which had gone on the rampage and stopped it from doing further damage. A fight with a large bully led to the name Mahavira or "Great Hero".

He almost certainly received the typical training of a prince of that period, e.g. in literature, political science, archery, mathematics, etc. He was very intelligent and at an early age his teacher confessed that Mahavira was ahead of him in knowledge.

He led a normal domestic life and married Yaśodā (that is according to Svetambara, but was not married according to Digambara), having a daughter named Priyadarśanā. According to one version, when he was 28 years old, on leaving the palace one day he saw a slave being whipped by his owner. Through this incident he became unhappy with the exploitation of the poor, ignorant and illiterate by richer members of the community, and a desire to leave family life developed within him. He did, however, have a deep feeling of consideration for his parents and this moved him to vow that he would not renounce domestic life until they had both passed away. After the death of his parents he waited until some two years later when their loss had become bearable to his elder brother, and then asked his permission to leave the palace. (The Digambaras believe that he became a monk while his parents were still alive.) It is believed that during these last two years in the palace he spent a considerable time in self-analysis, rather than in mundane, everyday pursuits.

He then left home to search for the root of all problems, i.e. to understand human nature and to study the universe in general. Obviously, his social status and environment whilst living in the palace was unsuited to this quest.

A.1.1 PURSUIT OF THE GOAL AND ENLIGHTENMENT

He devoted the subsequent twelve and a half years to his research with intense single-mindedness. As he felt that it would assist his meditation, he lived very frugally, wandering from place to place wearing only a single garment and frequently fasting. He also reduced his other needs, e.g. by removing his hair by hand. So intense was his concentration on his goal, that when his garment was accidentally caught on a thorn bush and pulled off, during 13 months of renunciation, he remained naked. (However, according to the Digambaras, he removed his clothes at the time of renunciation.)

Another incident showing his single-mindedness of purpose relates to how he was meditating in a standing posture in a farm and the farmer who had his cows grazing around him, asked him to look after them whilst he was away. Since he was in a state of deep meditation, Mahavira did not notice that the cows were wandering away. When the farmer came back, he asked Mahavira about the missing cows and since he was under a vow of silence, he did not reply. The already upset farmer was further infuriated and he hammered two wooden nails through Mahavira's ear to punish him for this lapse. But even that action did not break Mahavira's silence, and Mahavira remained compassionate towards him.

It is said that he remained in total solitude unil Mikkhali Gosāla, who had heard of Mahavira's outstanding abilities, searched and found him. Gosāla was a travelling story-teller and a follower of the fatalist doctrine of the Ājīvika sect of which he later became chief spokesman. It is related that they were together for six years during which time Gosāla became thoroughly acquainted with Mahavira and his abilities. Mahavira described the six months of austerities which he thought necessary for the attainment of these abilities.

Mahavira finally attained kevalajñāna (Dynamic Omniscience State) precisely 12 years, 6 months and 15 days after starting out on his search. Thus he was able to comprehend the mechanism of the universe as a whole and human nature in particular, which led him to the root of all problems.

A.1.2 CAREER AS A TIRTHANKARA

Having left his princely state in pursuit of his goal, on his enlightenment Mahavira came back to share his knowledge with the community. The event of coming back is far more significant than his search. He gave his first sermon to an audience which included Indrabhūti Gautama, who was well-versed in Hindu scriptures and extremely proud of his knowledge. Through this encounter Gautama became his chief disciple (gaṇadhara). Eventually he had eleven gaṇadharas as his inner circle. He had a great natural organisational ability and as his followers grew in number, he formed "*tīrtha*" (the order) of monks, nuns, laymen and laywomen. Also his daughter, Priyadarśanā, who was married to Jamāli, eventually became a follower of Mahavira.

To distinguish his ideas clearly from the prevalent influence of Hinduism, he developed a very versatile talent for coining new terminology, e.g. the lay followers were called śrāvaka, those who are attentive (right) listeners, and monks were called śramaṇa, that is, labourers on the spiritual path. He vigorously reaffirmed the concept of autonomous self-responsibility, that is, removing the idea of a God who influences the day to day activities of everyone. Further, he claimed "Every man has a right to and could attain nirvana by his own effort without the help of any supreme authority or mediatory priest."

He preached equality to all living beings, including the equality of all mankind, i.e. abandonment of slavery, the caste system, animal sacrifices etc. In fact, the leader of the order of nuns was a slave named Candanā. At the other extreme, one of the kings of that time, Bimbisāra, became a staunch follower. (See, H.L. Jain & Upadhye, 1974)

One of the revolutionary contributions of Mahavira was to change the Hindu recommendation that monkhood should not commence before the latter part of one's life. He introduced the idea that there is no particular time for worldly renunciation, with gradual transformation advocated for those who are not ready for total renunciation at an early age.

One of the outstanding features of Mahavira was that he was the perfect living image of compassion towards all forms of life. An example quoted is of a cobra called Chandkosiā, which had been withstanding all who had tried to cross its path. One day, the cobra bit Mahavira, but such was his knowledge that he could see, through the cobra's past lives, how it had developed such a nature and he had great compassion for it. Such was his compassion, rather like a mother for her child, that it was as though milk flowed through the wound and the injury became secondary to the concern that Mahavira had for the cobra's well-being.

Ultimately, Gosāla turned against Mahavira and challenging Mahavira, he tried to intimidate him with a curse, saying that he would die of a fever within six months. Mahavira did become ill but eventually recovered. The death of Gosāla shortly afterwards gave the impression that the curse had returned to its source. However, Mahavira himself was always against magical or Yogic power.

Mahavira continued to teach and practise the three jewels up to the time of his holy death. Various fundamental teachings and practices, with only minor variations, are still prevalent among Jains. In particular, all Jains celebrate the festival of lights (Diwali) because on Diwali's day Mahavira achieved Mokṣa, whereas on the same day his main disciple Gautama attained the omniscience state.

APPENDIX 2: JAIN SCRIPTURES

IT IS BELIEVED that the sermons of a Tirthankara take the form of what is known as the divine language/sound. (According to Digambaras, this sound transmits the intrinsic meaning of the teaching which is then translated into the scriptures by several chief disciples, "gaṇadharas", whereas according to Svetambara, the Tirthankara speaks in a divine human language.) In general, the role of the gaṇadharas was of translators/editors. Thus, one should not take the scripture literally, but keep in the forefront the idea of self-analysis and synthesis.

A.2.1 MAIN SCRIPTURES

In all there are 60 Jain scriptures (Āgamas) which are classified into three parts:—

Part I: Pūrva; Part II: Aṅga; Part III: Aṅgabāhya.

Out of these 60 texts, only 45 are still in existence. Table A.2.1 gives a skeleton of these texts with some details, whereas Table A.2.2 gives details for the sub-parts of Part III: Part IIIa,..., Part IIIe. Gautama and Sudharman, Mahavira's chief disciples (see, Appendix 1) have been the main contributors to the main twelve scriptures (Aṅgas) but the tradition of oral transmission was carried on for a long time.

The writing up of the canon with commentaries really began around 450 A.D. at the instigation of a council which was held in Valabhi. Bhadrabāhu II (fifth century) and Jinabhadra (sixth century) are two famous commentators.

Some of the important texts in the scriptures are as follows:

(A) *Ācārāṅga* (Part II). The law book of Jain monks and nuns dealing with their conduct.

(B) *Sūtrakṛtāṅga* (Part II). Gives a critical examination through non-absolutism (anekāntavāda) of the teaching opposed to Jain.

Table A.2.1 *Available main Scriptures of Jains with the total accepted scriptures given in brackets*

Number of texts	I Pūrva (old texts)	II Aṅgas (main texts)	III Aṅgabāhya* (Subsidiary texts)
Svetambara	0(14)	First 11(12)	34(34)
Sthanakvasi	0(14)	Same first 11(12)	21+(21+)
Tarapanthy	0(14)	Same first 11(12)	73(73)
Digambara	0(14)	Same first 11(12)	14(14)

* See Table A.2.2

Table A.2.2 *Some details of Part III: Aṅgabāhya of Table A.2.1*

Name	Meaning	Number of texts Svetambara	Stathankvasi
a Upāṅga	Subsidiary to Aṅga	12	Same 12
b Chedasūtra	Books of discipline	6	Same 6
c Mūlasūtra	Main scripture	4	1 of 4 *
d Prakīrṇakasūtra	The miscellaneous	10	(1 extracted from 10 ?)
e Cūlikāsūtra	Appendix	2	2

*Daśavaikālika.

(C) *Bhagavatī* (Part II). (Means the venerable.) Gives questions of Gautama and answers of Mahavira, with the use of the conditional dialectics (Syādvāda). Also the confrontation of Gosāla with Mahavira is recorded.

(D) *Dṛṣṭivāda* (Part II). This is the extinct Anga and it contained in particular sections on the doctrine of karmons which are transmitted in Digambara in their only canonical texts: *Ṣatkhaṇḍāgama* and *Kaṣāyaprābhṛta.* The most notable respective commentaries are of Virasena's *Dhavalā* (A.D. 800) and Jinasen's *Jayadhavalā* (A.D. 820). In Svetambara literature, a well-known commentary on the doctrine of karmons is in Devendrasuri's *Karmagrantha* (14th century); for a list of its contents in English see Glasenapp (1942).

(E) *Ācāradaśāḥ* (Part IIIb). Kalpa-sūtra is another important work which is the eigth chapter of Ācāradaśāḥ appended with a collected biography of Tirthankaras and the lineage of successors to the gaṇadharas: the eighth chapter gives the rules for monastic life during the rainy season. This has been used in public recitation for over 1500 years [especially during Paryūṣhaṇa—a ten-day (Digambara)/eight-day (Svetambara) holy period of Jain] ever since it was chanted before King Dhruvasena of Valabhi to comfort him on the death of his son.

(F) *Daśavaikālika* (Part IIIc). Contains topics on the monastic life. However, the ten lectures which it contains are to be studied beyond the prescribed hours.

(G) *Uttarādhyayana* (Part IIIc). This work (book of later instructions) is claimed to be the last sermon of Mahavira, especially the advice of Mahavira to Gautama on non-attachment to his teacher. Also, it contains the dialogue between Keśi and Gautama on increasing the number of vows from 4 to 5 in Mahavira's time. The appended fifth vow is regarding celibacy.

(H) *Āvaśyaka* (Part IIIc). Contains most of the content of the present Pratikramaṇa Sūtra (ritualised confession) still in usage which summarises Jain teaching.

A.2.2 SECONDARY SCRIPTURES

The secondary scriptures (Ānuyogas) supplement the older material and there are four parts just as if they were the four Vedas of the Jains. These were mostly written by monk scholars:

(1) *Prathamānuyoga* (the primary exposition) deals with biographies of Tirthankaras.

(2) *Karaṇānuyoga* (exposition on technical matters) deals with ancient sciences such as cosmology and astrology.

(3) *Caraṇānuyoga* (exposition on discipline) is the most important work on Jain Yogas. It includes Hemacandra's Yogaśāstra (twelfth century) and Haribhadra's Dharmabindu (eighth century).

(4) *Dravānuyoga* (exposition on existents) includes the most important work, Tattvārtha-sūtra of Umāsvāti (second century). This work summarized concisely the whole of the Jain doctrinal system into about 350 verses. It is comparable to Patañjali's Yogasūtra by presenting the teaching in an integrated philosophical school. Other works included are of

Siddhasena Divākara's Nyāyāvatara and Sanmati-sūtra (5th century) which are excellent works of logic. Yaśovijaya (eighteenth century) represents the modern school of logic.

Our discussion is somewhat restricted to Svetambara. Digambara also believes that there were 60 texts with the above titles but believes that they are all lost. They possess some record leading to two important scriptures of the second century:- Ṣatkhaṇḍāgama (scriptures in six parts), and Kaṣāyaprābhṛta (Four-Passions—'Gifts'). The work of Kundakunda (perhaps second century) is the most comprehensive which includes Samayasāra, Niyamasāra and Pravacanasāra. His tradition was continued in the sixth century by Pūjyapāda. The important commentary "Ātmakhyāti" on Samayasāra by Amṛtacandra appeared in the eleventh century. Other representative writers to be mentioned are Jinasena (ninth century) and Somadeva (tenth century). Appropriate versions of Umāsvāti's work "Tattvārtha-sūtra" (as well as Siddhasena's work on logic) are accepted by both sects. For further details, we refer to P.S. Jaini (1979, Ch. 2).

The first group of Āgama scriptures were written in Ardha Māgadhī which was a Prakrit dialect of Magadha. The subsequent works are in Sanskrit, starting from the work of Umāsvāti. Thus, there is a vast literature available but it seems that Tattvārtha-sūtra of Umāsvāti can be regarded as the main philosophical text of the religion and is recognised as authoritative by all Jains. It should be noted that a compilation of 756 verses representing the sum and substance of Jain scriptures of Digambara as well as Svetambara tradition appeared under the title of SAMAN SUTTAM. It was published by Sarva Seva Sangh (Rajghat, Varanasi) on the occasion of 2500th anniversary of Mahavira's nirvana on April 24, 1975, and in 1993 the publisher has printed its English translation. Part A of the Bibliography gives references to translations of a few important works.

APPENDIX 3: CITATIONS

A. *Axioms.* (v = verse)

Axiom 1.
Jīva ity ... karma-sayūnkataḥ,
(Pañcāstikaya-Sāra, v. 27)
Yathā-pravṛtta-karaṇam ity arthaḥ,
(Viśeṣāvaśyaka-bhāṣya, v. 1202)

Axiom 2.
Nārkatīryaṅ manuṣyā devā ity nāmsanyotaḥ prakratyah.
(Pañcāstikaya-Sāra, v. 55)
(*cf.* "karmāvaran mātrāyāḥ, tāratmya vibhedataḥ". Nathmal, 1970, Ch. 2. v. 63).

Axiom 3.
Pariṇāmātkarma karmaṇo bhavati gatiṣu gatiḥ.
(Pañcāstikaya-Sāra, v. 128)

Axiom 4A.
Mithyādarśana avirati pramāda kaṣāya yogāḥ bandhahetavaḥ.
(Tattvārtha-sūtra, Ch. 8, v. 1)

Axiom 4B.
... Prāṇīghātten .... saptaṃ narkan gatoh,
Mātev serva bhūttānāmahiṃsa hitakārinī,
Ahiṃsāyaḥ phalaṃ sarva, kimnyataḥ, kāmdaiva sah.
(Yogaśāstra, Ch. 2, vs. 27, 51, 52)

Axiom 4C.
Tapsā nirjarā ca.
(Tattvārtha-sūtra, Ch. 9, v. 3)

B. *Texts* (Quotation = q)

q 3.1 Savve karei jīvo ajjhavasāṇeṇa tiriyaṇeraie,
devamaṇuve ya savve puṇṇaṁ pāvaṁ ca aṇeyavihaṁ.
(Samayasāra, v. 268)

q 5.1 Śubhaḥ puṇyasyāśubhaḥ pāpasya.
(Tattvārtha-sūtra, Ch .6, v. 3)

q 5.2 Sakaṣāyatvājjīvaḥ karmaṇo ... sa bandhaḥ.
(Tattvārtha-sūtra, Ch. 8, v. 2)

q 6.1 Parspropagraho jīvānām
(Tattvārtha-sūtra, Ch. 5, v. 21)

q 6.2 Purisa! tummev tuṃ mitraḥ, kiṃ bahiya mitramitcchasi.
(Ācārāṅga-sūtra, Ch. 3, v. 125)

q 6.3 Savve jīvā vi icchanti jīvium na marijjiuṃ
(Daśavaikālikā-sūtra, Ch. 6, v. 10)

q 6.4 Mā pamāyae.
(Uttarādhyayana-sūtra, Ch .10, v. 1)

q 6.5 Matrī pramoda kāruṇyamādhyasthāni ca
sattva guṇādhika kliśyamānā vineyeṣu.
(Tattvārthā-sutra, Ch. 7, v. 6)

q 7.1 Jānaṇ balābalam.
(Yogaśāstra, Ch. 1, v. 54)

q 8.1 Sa gupti samiti dharmānuprekṣā purīṣahjaya cāritraiḥ.
(Tattvārtha-sūtra, Ch. 9, v. 2)

q 8.2 Ṇāṇeṇ jāṇi bhāve daṇsṇeṇ ya suddadahe;
caritṛeṇ ṇiginhai taveṇ parisujji.
(Uttarādhyayana-sūtra, Ch. 28, v. 35)

q 8.3 Samyag darśana jñāna cāritrāṇi mokṣa mārgaḥ.
(Tattvārtha-sūtra, Ch. 1, v. 1)

q 8.4 Prathamaṃ jñānaṃ. tato dayā
(Daśavaikālika-sūtra, Ch. 4, v. 10)

q 8.5 Māse māse tu jo bālo kūsggeṇ tu bhuṇje;
ṇa so sūykkhāy dhammassa kalaṇ agghai solasiṇ.
(Uttarādhyayana-sūtra, Ch. 9, v. 44)

APPENDIX 4: PURIFICATION STAGES AND A GAME OF SNAKES AND LADDERS

THE PRESENT AUTHOR has invented a modified form of the game of snakes and ladders to represent the key transitions between the purification stages (see, Fig. A.4.1). The playing board has sixteen squares and moves are made after tossing a coin: a 'tail' scores 1 and a 'head' scores 2. The first two squares on the board represent lower life and higher life in the animal kingdom respectively.

At square 3 we have the human form ready to ascend from its first stage, step by step, to the higher stages. The rules of the game are:

(a) to begin a tail must be thrown; and
(b) at square 2 a tail must be thrown; this takes the player to square 3 and hence up the ladder to stage (3).

Note that it is not permitted to move from square 2 to square 4 by throwing a 'head'. The player can only occupy square 4 by arriving at stage (7) and falling down the snake. The end of the game must be exact, i.e. a player on stage (13) must throw a 'tail'.

In view of the case of a Mahavira's disciple (Ānanda) it is possible to take a ladder from stage (5) to stage (8), i.e. without passing through the stage of being a monk. In general, the game emphasises where progress (ladders) can occur where downfalls (snakes) can take place. Once stage 12 has been reached one can always reach stage (14) and then attain mokṣa.

An early version of such a quasi-religious game is called *Jñānabāzi* (the game of knowledge). See for an illustration as well as further details in Pal (1994, p. 87).

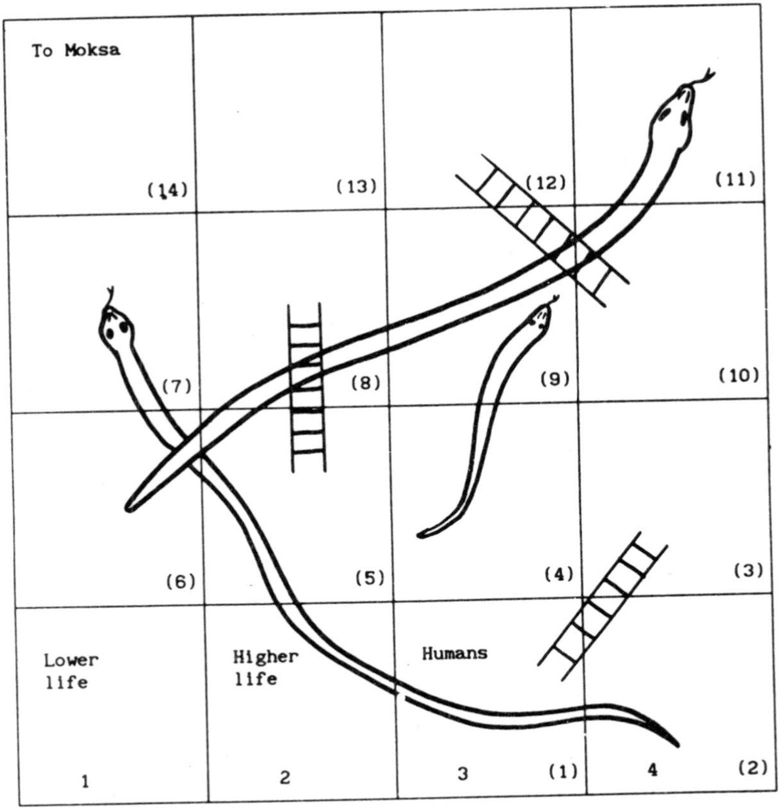

Fig. A.4.1 Transitions illustrated through snakes and ladders, (X) denotes the stage X of purification.

Rules:

(a) a tossed coin scores 1 for a 'tail' and 2 for a 'head';
(b) begin with a 'tail' only: this puts the counter on 1;
(c) if a 'tail' is thrown next, put the counter on 2, then another 'tail' must be thrown—taking the counter to square 3 and up the ladder to stage (3);
(d) square 4 is barred, except for a fall from stage (7).

BIBLIOGRAPHY

A. TEXTS AND TRANSLATIONS

Ācārāṅga-sūtra. Prakrit text and Hindi translation by Madhukar Muni, Shri Āgam Prakāshan Samiti, Beawar, 1980

______tr. by H. Jacobi in *Jaina Sūtras,* Vol. 1, 1-213, reprinted Dover Publications, New York, 1968

Āvassaya-sutta. Jain Agama Series No.15, Shri Mahavir Jain Vidyalaya, Bombay, 1977

Daśavaikālika-sūtra. tr. by K.C. Lalwani, Motilal Banarsidass, Delhi, 1973

Kalpa-sūtra. translated by H. Jacobi in *Jaina Sūtras,* Vol. 2, 217-311, reprinted Dover Publications, New York, 1968

Karmagrantha of Devendrasūri, Parts 1-6 tr. (Hindi) by Singhvi, S.L., Vardhman Sthanakvasi Jain, Dharmic Siksha Samiti, Badot (Merrut), 1984

Mahāpurāṇu of Puṣpandanta, 3 pts., Apabhraṃśa text ed. by P.L. Vaidya. Manikchandra Digambara Jaina Granthamala, Bombay, 1937-47

Pancastikaya-sara of Kundakunda, Prakrit text, Sanskrit chaya with English tr. by Chakravarti, A. & Upadhye, Bhāratīya Jñānpītha Publication, Delhi, 1975

Pravacanasāra of Kundakunda (With Amṛtacandra's Tāttvadīpikā, Jayasena's) Tātparya-vṛtti and Pāṇḍe Hemarāja's Bālāva-bodha-bhāṣāṭīkā), ed. with tr. of *Pravacanasāra* by A.N. Upadhye (Rajacandra Jaina Śāstramālā Agas) 1934

Saman Sutam (1993). Sarva Seva Sangh, Rajghat, Varanasi.

Samayasāra of Kundakunda (with Amṛtacandra's Ātmakhyāti-ṭīkā). Prakrit text and translation by A. Chakravarti, Bhāratīya Jñānapītha Publication, Delhi, 2nd edition, 1971

Tattvārtha-sūtra of Umāsvāti, Sanskrit text with Pt. Sukhlalji's Commentary tr. by K.K. Dixit, L.D. Institute of Indology, Ahmedabad, 1974; tr. by Nathmal Tatia, *"That Which Is."* Harper Collins, 1994. The Sacred Literature Series

Uttarādhyayana-sūtra. Prakrit text and tr. by K.C. Lalwani, Prajnanam, Calcutta, 1977; tr. by H. Jacobi in *Jaina Sūtras,* Vol. 2, 1-232, reprinted Dover Publications, New York, 1968

Viśeṣāvaśyaka-bhāṣya of Jinabhadragaṇi, Vol. 1, ed. by Nathmal Tatia, Research Institute of Prakrit, Jainology and Ahiṃsā Vaishali, 1972

Yogaśāstra of Hemacandra, Sanskrit text with Hindi tr. by Muni Padamvijay, Shri Nirgranth Sāhitya Prakāṣansang, Delhi, 1975

B. MODERN WORKS

Amarendravijay (1993) *Science Discovers Eternal Wisdom.* Jain Sahitya Academy, Gandhidham

Basham, A.L. (1958) "Jainism and Buddhism." *Sources in Indian Tradition,* ed. de Bary, W.T. Vol. 1, 38-92, Columbia Univ. Press, New York

Bharucha, F. (1993) *Role of Space-Time in Jaina's Syādvāda and Quantum Theory,* Sri Satguru Publications, Delhi

Capra, F. (1975) *Tao of Physics.* Wildwood House, Hounslow

Carrithers, M. & Humphrey, C. (1991) *The Assembly of Listeners, Jains in Society,* Cambridge University Press, Cambridge

Chitrabhanu, Gurudev Shree (1980) *Twelve Facets of Reality: The Jain Path of Freedom.* (Edited by Clare Rosenfield) Dodd, Mead & Co. New York

Davies, P.C.W. (1983) *God and the New Physics.* London: J.M. Dent; Penguin Books (1984)

Dundas, P. (1992) *The Jains,* Routledge, London

Einstein, A (1940) Science and Religion, *Nature,* Vol. **146**, pp. 605-7.

Einstein, A. (1941) "Science and Religion" First conference on Science, Philosophy and Religion, New York (Reprinted in *Ideas and Opinions,* 1973, Souvenir Press, London)

d'Espagnat, B. (1979) "The quantum theory and reality," *Scientific American,* **241**, pp. 128-40

Gamow, G. (1965) *Mr. Tompkins in Paperback.* Cambridge Univ. Press

von Glasenapp, H. (1942) *The Doctrine of Karma in Jain Philosophy.* tr. from the German by G. Barry Gifford. Bai Vijibhai Jivanlal Pannalal Charity Fund, Bombay

Gribbin, J. (1984) *In Search of Schrödinger's Cat* Wildwood House (Reprinted by Corgi books)

Haldane, J.B.S. (1957) "The syādvāda system of predication." *Sankhyā,* **A 18**, pp. 195-200

Hawking, S.W. (1988) *A Brief History of Time.* Bantam Press, London

Hay, S.N. (1970) "Jain influences on Gandhi's early thought" in *Gandhi, India and the World,* ed. S. Ray, pp. 29-38. Philadelphia: Temple Univ. Press

Jacobi, Hermann (1884, 1895) *Jaina Sutras,* Vol. 1, 2, Sacred Books of the East, XXII, XLV; Oxford. Reprinted (1968), Dover Publications, New York

Jahn, R.G. (1982) "The persistent paradox of psychic phenomena: an engineering perspective." Proc. Inst. of Elec. & Electronics Engr., 70 pp. 136-70

Jain, D.C. (1990) (Editor) *Studies in Jainism.* Jain Study Circle, Flushing, New York

Jain, C.R. (1929) *The Practical Dharma.* The Indian Press, Allahabad (Reprinted as *Fundamentals of Jainism,* 1974, Veer Nirvan Bharti, Meerut)

Jain, G.R. (1975) *Cosmology Old and New.* Bhāratīya Jñānpītha Publication, Delhi

Jain, H.L. and Upadhye, A.N. (1974) *Mahavira: his Times and his Philosophy of Life.* Bhāratīya Jñānpītha Publication, Delhi

Jain, L.C. (1992) *The Tao of Jaina Sciences.* Arihant International, Delhi

Jain, N.L. (1993) *Jain Systems in Nutshell.* Nij-Jnan-Sagar Shiksha Kosha, Satna

Jain, S.K. (1980) "Communication regarding the process of rebirth" in *Karma and Rebirth in Classical Indian Traditions* ed. by W.D. O'Flaherty. pp. 237-8. Univ. of California Press, Berkeley

Jaini, J.L. (1916) *Outlines of Jainism.* Cambridge. Reprinted in 1979. J.L. Jaini Trust, Indore

Jaini, P.S. (1979) *The Jaina Path of Purification.* Univ. of California Press: Berkeley (Reprinted by Motilal Banarsidass, Delhi)

______ (1991) *Gender and Salvation.* University of California Press, Berkeley

Kapashi, V. (1985) *Jainism for Young Persons.* Jain Samaj Publications, Leicester

Kapashi, V., Shah, A. and Desai, K. (1994) *Text Book of Jainism : Level I.* Institute of Jainology, London

Khursheed, A. (1987) *Science and Religion.* One World Publication, London

King, Ursula (1987) "Jainism." In *The Encyclopedia of World Faiths.* ed. Bishop, P. and Darton, M. Macdonald Orbis 1987, London and Sydney

Kothari, D.S. (1975) "Some Thoughts on Truth". Anniversary Address, *Indian National Science Academy,* pp.1-23, Delhi

Mahalanobis, P.C. (1954) "The Foundations of Statistics." *Dialectica* **8**, pp. 95-111

Mardia, K.V. (1975) "Jain logic and statistical concepts." *Jain Antiquary and Jaina Siddhanta Bhaskar.* Oriental Research Institute, Arrah, **27**, pp. 33-7

______(1976) *Do-it-Yourself Statistical Analysis.* Leeds University Review, **19**, pp. 79-98

______(1981) "Why Paryushana is doing your own MOT?" *The Jain,* **3**, issue 9, pp. 4-5

______(1982) "Mahavira as a man." *The Jain, 4,* issue 11, p. 16

______(1988a) Discussion to "Probability, Statistics and Theology", by D.J. Bartholomew. *J. Roy. Statist.* Soc **A 151**, pp. 166-7

______(1988b) "Jain Culture." *The Jain,* Pratistha Mahotsava Souvenir Issue, pp. 51-3. Jain Samaj Publications, Leicester.

______(1991) "Modern science and the principle of karmons in Jainism." *Jain Journal,* Vol. **26**, pp. 116-19

______(1992) *Jain Thoughts and Prayers,* The Yorkshire, Jain Foundation, Leeds

Marett, P. (1985) *Jainism Explained,* Jain Samaj Europe Publications, Leicester

Matilal, B.K. (1981) *The Central Philosophy of Jainism* (Anekanta-vāda) L.D. Institute of Indology, Ahmedabad

Mehta, M.L. (1995) *Jaina Psychology,* Sohanlal Jaindharma Pracharak Samiti; Amritsar

Nandighoshvijay, Munishri (1995), *Jainism : Through Science,* Shri Mahavira Jain Vidyalaya, Bombay.

Nathmal, Muni (1970) *Wisdom of Mahavira,* tr. Bhuteria, K. and Manian, K.S., Adarṣ Sāhitya Sangh Publication, Churu

Oldfield, K. (1989) *Jainism: The Path of Purity and Peace.* Christian Education Movement, Derby

Pal, P. (1994) *The Peaceful Liberators: Jain Art from India,* Thames and Hudson, Los Angeles Country Museum of Art

Pedler, K. (1981) *Mind over Matter.* Thomas Methuen, London

Popper, K.R. (1968) *The Logic of Scientific Discovery.* 2nd ed. Hutchinson, London

Shah, A.K. (1991) *Experiments with Jainism.* Young Jains Publications, London

Shah, B.S. (1992) *An Introduction to Jainism.* The Setubandh Publications, New York

Sheldrake, R. (1981) *A New Science of Life.* Blond & Briggs Ltd. (Paladin Books, 1983)

Singhvi, L.M. (1990) *The Jain Declaration on Nature.* The Jain Sacred Literature Trust, London

Stevenson, S. (1915) *The Heart of Jainism.* Oxford Univ. Press. Reprinted in 1970. Motilal Banarsidass, Delhi (also see, review *The Jain,* 1983, pp. 5-6)

Tatia, N. (1984) *New Dimensions in Jaina Logic.* tr. of "Jaina Nyaya ka Vikasa" Mahaprajna Yuvācārysaāi. Jaina Vishva Bharati, Ladnun

______(1986) *Jaina Meditation Citta: Samādhi: Jaina-Yoga.* Jaina Vishva Bharati, Ladnun

Tobias, M. (1991) *LifeForce.* (The World of Jainism) Asian Humanities Press, Berkeley

Vakharia, N.N. (1978) *Cosmological Truths of Ancient Indian Religions Jainism and Hinduism.* Flint, Michigan

Williams, R. (1963) *Jaina Yoga: A Survey of the Mediaeval Sravakacaras.* Oxford University Press, London (Reprint, Motilal Banarsidass, 1983)

Wilson, I. (1981) *Mind out of Time?* Gollancz, London

Zaveri, J.S. (1975) *Theory of Atom in the Jaina Philosophy.* Jaina Vishva Bharati, Ladnun

INDEX TO GLOSSARY

Abhāsa (fallacy), 95
Ācārya (Spiritual master), 26
Ācārāṅga (a scripture), 121, 126
Adharma (Dynamic medium; a dravya), 41
Āgamas (Jain scriptures), 121
Aghātiyā (Secondary Karmic Component), 41
Ahiṁsā (Non-violence/harmlessness), 60, 90
Ajīva (Non-soul/Insentient object), 19, 26
Ākāśa (Space; a dravya), 41
Aloka-Ākāśa (unoccupied space; a dravya), 41
Amūḍhadṛṣṭi (Freedom from false notions), 90
Anekāntavāda (Jain Holistic Principle), 93-94, 99, 113
Aṅga (Jain scriptures, main texts), 121
Aṅgabāhya (Jain scriptures, subsidiary texts), 121
Anitya (impermanent; an Anuprekṣa), 90
Anivṛtti-Samparava (Uniformly Mild Volition); a *Gunasthana*, 76
Anubhava (Potential energy in karmon—decay), 19
Anu Brahmavrata (no sexual deviations), 90
Anuprekṣa (Reflections; Twelve kinds), 90
Anuvrata (Five Lower Vows) 90
Ānuyoga (Secondary Scripture), 123
Anyatva, (separateness; an Anuprekṣa), 90
Aparigraha (Non-possession), 90
āpo-kāyika (water-bodies), 27
Apramatta-virata (Enlightened world view with careless restraint; a *Gunasthana*), 76
Apūrva-karaṇa (unprecedented spiritual progress; a *Gunasthana*), 76
Ārambhajā-himsā (Accidental/occupational violence), 60
Arihaṇta (Perfect being) 19, 26
Ārtadhyāna (mournful meditation), 90
Asarava (helplessness; an Anuprekṣa), 90
Asātā-vedanīya (karmic component, secondary, pain producing), 41
Āsarava (Karmic force/influx; an Anuprekṣa), 19, 90
Aṣṭāṅga (Eight qualities of the True Insight), 90
Asteya (No-stealing), 90
Asucya (impurity; an Anuprekṣa), 90
Avadhijñana (clairvoyance), 93-94, 100
Avasarpiṇī (regressive half-cycle), 60
Āvaśyaka (scripture), 123
Avirati (Non-restraint), 51
Ayoga-kevalin (static omniscience state; a *Gunasthana*), 76
Āyu (karmic component, secondary, longevity determining), 41

Bandha (Karmic bondage / fusion), 19
Bhāva (Volition), 51
Bhavyatva [Freedom longing (catalyst)], 19
Bodhi-durlabha, (the rarity of true insight; an Anuprekṣa), 90

Cāritra-Mohanīya (karmic component, conduct deluding), 41
Caranānkyoga (a scripture), 123

Darśana-āvaraṇīya (karmic component: perception obscuring), 41
Darśana-Mohanīya (karmic component: insight deluding), 41
Darśana (Perception), 19
Daśa-Dharma (Ten-fold Righteousness), 90
Daśavaikālika (a scripture) 123, 126
Deśa-virata (partial self-restraint; a *Gunasthana*), 76
Deva (Heavenly being), 27
Dharma (Righteousness), 90; (Stationary Medium; a Dravya), 41
Dharmadhyāna (Virtuous Meditation), 90
Dharma-svākhyātatva (Jain teaching; an Anuprekṣa), 90
Dhyānas (Meditation), 90
Digambara (a Jain school; monks 'sky-clad'), 5-6, 8
Dravānuyoga (a scricpture), 123
Dravya (Existents; Six Kinds), 41
Duṣamā (misery/unhappiness), *see kala*
Dveṣa (Aversion), 51

Ekatva (aloneness; Anuprekṣa), 90

Gati (Four Existences), 27
Ghātīya (primary karmic components), 41
Gotra (karmic component; environmental determining), 41
Guna (soul's element), 19
Guṇasthānas (Fourteen purification stages), 76
Gupti (restraint), 90; kāyā (body), 90; mana (mind), 90; vachan (speech), 90

Hiṁsā (Violence) 60

Jai Jinendra (honour to Jina), 1
Jina (Tirthankara), 1
Jiva (soul, a Dravya), 41; (Soul), 18; (Soul/living being), 10, 26
Jñāna (Knowledge), 19
Jñānā-avaraṇīya (karmic component: knowledge obscuring), 41

Karaṇānuyoga (a scripture), 123
Kāla (time; a Dravya), 41
Kāla (Temporal Cycles), 60; Utsarpiṇī (Progressive half-cycle), 60; Avasarpiṇī (Regressive half-cycle), 51; Suṣamā (Happy), 60; Duṣamā (Misery/unhappy), 60
Kalpaintra (a scripture), 60
Karma (Karmic matter, composed of karmic particles), 16, 19
karma (Eight karmic components), 41
kamagrantha, 122
kārmic Śarīra (types of bodies), *see śarīra*
Kaṣāya [Four Passions (principal)], 51
kāyā (body), 90
Kevaljñāna (infinite omniscience knowledge), 100
Krodha (anger), 51
Ksināmoha (completely eliminated greed; a *Gunasthana*), 76

Leśya (karmic stain on soul), 114
Lobha (greed), 51
Loka Ākāsa (unoccupied space, a *dravya*), 41
Loka-ākāśa, (universe; Anuprekṣa), 90

Mahāvīra (24th Tirthankara), 1, 2, 3, 6 life of, 117-20
Mahapuranu, 15
mana (mind), 90
Māna (pride), 51
Manahparyaya jñāna (mind reading), 100
Matijñāna (empirical knowledge), 100
Manuṣya (Humane), 27
Māyā (deceit), 51
Mokṣa (Liberation; an Anuprekṣa), 19, 90
Mishra (Mixture of Deluded and Enlightened World View; a *Gunasthana*), 76

Mithyādarśana, 51
Mithyādṛṣṭi (Deluded World View; a *Gunasthana*), 76
Mohanīya (karmic component: bliss-defiling), 41
Mokṣa, 19, 90
Muh-paṭṭi (Mouth mask), 8
Mūrcchā (attachment, a state of trance), 114

Nāma (karmic component: body producing), 41
Nāraki (Hellish being), 27
Nayavāda (Unique standpoint principle), 99
Nigoda (Micro-organisms), 26
Nikṣepa (Classification of imports of words), 99
Niḥkāṃkṣita (Freedom from anticipation), 90
Niḥsāṁksita (Freedom from doubt), 90
Nirjarā (Karmic fission/decay; an Anuprekṣa), 19, 90
Nirvicikitsā (Freedom from disgust), 90
No-Kasāya (Subsidiary Passions). 51

Pañca-parameṣṭhin (Five-spiritually high), 26
Pāpa (Heavy karmic matter), 19
Paramāṇu (Ultimate Particle), 41
Parigraha (possession), 81, 85, 113
Parīsahajaya (Afflictions mastery), 90
Pārśva (23rd Tirthankara), 1, 3, 5, 6
Prabhāvanā (Illumination), 90
Pradeśa (Space point), 41
Pradeśa (Number of karmons in karmic fusion), 19
Prakṛti (Karmic components of karmic force), 19
Pramāda (Carelessness) 51
Pramāna (Comprehensive Right Knowledge), 93-94, 98
Pramattāvirata (E.W.V. with Careless S.R.), 76
Prathmānuyoga (a scripture), 123
Pratimā (renunciation stages), 90
Pṛthvī-kāyika (earth bodies), 27
Pudgala (matter; a Dravya), 35, 41, 102, 112
Puṇya (Light karmic matter), 19
Pūrva (Jain scriptures, old texts), 122

Rāga (attachment), 51
Ṛṣabha 1, 3, 7
Rutradhyāna (wrathful meditation), 90

Sādhu (Saint), 26
Samyak-cāritra (Right Conduct), 90
Samyak-dṛṣṭi Avirat (Non-restrained enlightened world view; a *Gunasthana*), 76
Samyak-jñāna (Right Knowledge), 90
Samiti (Watchfulness), 90
Samkalpajā-hiṁsā (Premeditated violence), 60
Samyak-darśana (Right Faith), 90
Samvara (Karmic force sheild; an Anuprekṣa), 19, 90
Saptabhangi-naya (The seven-fold conditional predication), 99
Sāsvādana (Lingering E.W.V.), 76
Śarīra (Type of bodies), 41 Kārmic Śarīra (Karmic body), 41 Taijas Śarīra (Karmic capsule), 41
Sata-vedanīya (Karmic component: pleasure producing), 41
Satya (Truthfulness), 90
Sayoga-kevalin (dynamic omniscience state; a *Gunasthana*), 76
Siddha (Liberated soul), 19, 26
Śrāvaka (Jain Layman), 90, 119
Śramana (monks), 119
Śrutajñāna (verbal/articulate knowledge), 100
Sthāṇakavāsi (a Jain sub-school of Svetambara; non-temple believer), 6, 122
Sthiti (Time to decay of fused karmons), 19
Sthitikaraṇa (Promoting stability),

Sthitikaraṇa (Promoting stability), 90
Sukha (Bliss), 19
Śukladhyāna (Pure Trance), 90
Suksma-moha (with subtle greed; a *Gunasthana*), 76
Suṣamā (happiness), *see kala*
Sūtrakṛtāṅga (a scripture), 121
Śvetāmbara (a Jain school; monk white-clad), 5-6
syādasti (maybe it is), 99
syādasti ca avaktavyaśca (maybe it is and is indeterminate), 100
syādasti nāsti ca (maybe it is and is not), 100
syādasti nāsti ca avaktavyaśca (maybe it is, is not and is indeterminate), 100
Syādvāda (Conditional Predication Principle), 95-96, 99, 112
syādavaktavyah (maybe it is indeterminate), 100
Syādavaktavyah (maybe it is indeterminate), 100
syāt (Maybe), 100
syātnāsti (maybe it is not), 99
syātnāsti cad avktavyaśca (maybe it is not and is indeterminate), 100

Taijas Śarīra (karmic capsule), *see* śarīra
Tāraṇapantha (a Jain sub-school of Digambara; non-temple believers), 6
Tattva (nine reals), 18
Tattvārtha-sūtra, 4, 93, 125-26
tejo-kāyika (fire bodies), 27
Terāpantha (a sub-school of Svetambara), 6
Tirthankara (omniscient spiritual teacher), 1,8
Tīryañca (Animal/Plant life), 27
tri-ratna (Three Jewels), 90

Udaya (Emission), 19
Upādhayāya (spiritual teacher), 26
Upagūhana (Safeguarding), 90
Upaśama (Suppression), 19
Upsanta-moha (partially complete self-restraint with supressed greed; a *Gunasthana*), 76
Utsarpiṇī (progressive half-cycle), *see kala*
Uttaradhyayana (a scripture), 123, 126

vachan (speech), 90
Vargaṇā (Particale-Groupings), 41
Vātsalya (Disinterested love), 90
Vāyu-kāyika (air bodies), 27
Vedanīya (karmic component: feeling producing), 41
Virodhi-hiṁsā (Defensive violence), 60
Vīrya (Energy), 19
Vīrya-antarāya (karmic component: energy ob structing), 41

Yoga (Activities of body, mind and speech), 51

GENERAL INDEX

Ācāradaśāh, 122
Ācāranga, 121, 126
a-component, *see* bliss-defiling component; *see* karmic component
actuality view, 94
afflictions, mastery of, 83
Ājīvikā, sect, 118
air-bodies, 23, 27
alcohol, 55
aloneness, 82
Amṛtacandra, 124
Amrendravijay, ix
analogies: elephant and the blind men in holistic principle, 96-98; the Four Passions in a driver, 87-89; karmic matter as a virus, 18; nuclear reactor and karmic reactor, 63; polluted soul as a magnet, 17-18; purity of the soul and gold, 9; purity of the soul and petrol, 18; purification stages with production of ghee, 87,
anger, 46-47, 50, 55, 72-73; degrees, 46-47; in driving, 89; in four passions, 46; in purification stages, 65; time period, 50; *see* passions, the four
animal, 23, 26-27
animal welfare, 109
animalistic state, 25-26
apassiono, 107
apple, 23, 112
Aristotle, 3-4, 95
atom, *see* particle
attitude: charitable, 50; and innerself, 68
austerity, 63, 64, 113; one of the rules of righteousness, 79; right conduct, 85-86
axioms, 6-7; axiom-1, 9; axiom-2, 21; axiom-3, 29; axiom-4A, 43; axiom-4B, 53; axiom-4C, 63

baryon, 103, 106
Basham, A.L., 30, 34-35, 109
Bhagavati, 122
Bhadrabahu, 121
Bharucha F., 96
big-bang, 109
Bimbisara, 119
Black hole and mokṣa, 38, 109, 110
bliss, 4; defiling of, 11, 14, 44; defiling karmic component, 29; effect of, 38, 44; element of the soul, 10; infinite, 10, 14, 45, 63; soul's purity, 10; vs pleasure, 25; vs. matter, 37
body, 18, 22, 23; karmic, *see karmic body*
body-producing karmic component (f-component), 30-31, 41; effect of, 44
boson, 103, 105-107
Buddha, 1, 3

Candana, 119
Capra, F., 41
capsule, karmic, 35-36; luminous 32-33, 41
Caranānuyoga, 123
carelessness 43; degrees, 69, 71; —free, 65, 70, 73, 76, 84; as hindrance to the path, 44; overcoming, 64, 69, 77; as karmic agent, 43; in purification stage, 69
chance, *see* uncertainty
Chandkosia, cobra, 120
Chedasūtra, 122
Chitrabhanu, Gurudev, 56, 82
Clairvoyance, 93-94, 100
Colours, 50; in Jaina particle physics, 38, 108; in modern physics, 105, 108
compassion, 10, 56, 68, 86
Complete self-restraint (C.S.R.) 65, 69-71, 76
Component, Karmic, *see* karmic com-

ponent
Concomitance, 94
Conditional predication Principle *see* Predications, Conditional
Conduct, right, 4, 44, 79, 85-86; as one of the three jewels, 85; deluding/defiling component, 30, 41, 44; practical effect of, 44
Cosmos, 111
Criminal, 22-23, 40
cycle, birth and death, 29; destructible components, 30; liberation of soul from, 40, 70; life axis, 39; reflections, 82, implications of, 40; Jain universal, 58, 59, 70

Darwin, 102
Davies, P.C.W., 110
decay, 7, 30; *see* karmic decay
deceit, 46; in purification stages, 69; in driving, 87, 89; *see* passions, the four
deluded world-view, 65, 67, 76
De Montfort University, ix
Devendrasuri, 122
Digambara, 5-6, 117
Divakara, 124
Diwali, 120
dynamic; medium, 34, 35, 41, 102; karmic process 11, 12, 48, 49, 66; forces, 35, 46; non-violence, 54; omniscience, 65, 70, 71, 76, 84, 119

earth-bodies, 22, 27
e-component, *see* feeling producing component
Einstein. A., vi, 102, 110-111, 113
electromagnetic force, 105, 111
elementary particles; Jain 36; modern physics, 101-03
energy, 10, 18-19, 21, 31, 66, potential in karmic decay, 14; of soul, 33, 35, 43, 46, 63, 84; obstructing component, 30, 41; and matter, 35, 36, 102; four passions, 66
Enlightened World-View (E.W.V.), 65, 67, 68, 70, 75, 76
enlightenment, of Mahavira, 118
environmental determining karmic component (h-component), 30, 31, 41, 45
equilibrium, 25; long-term state of, 14; stationary medium 33, 89, 102-03
d'Espagnat, B., 101
etymological view, 94
evolution, 17, 102
exchangeability, of matter and energy, 102
existents; holistic principle, 96; nine reals, 15; six, 33

faith right, 4, 85; lingering, 66, 67, 76; as one of the three jewels, 85, 90; Einstein's, 110
f-component, *see* body-producing component
feeling-producing karmic component (c-component), 30, 41; effect of, 44
Feynman diagrams, 106
fig, 55
fine, fine-fine, fine-gross, 35, 36
fire-bodies, 23, 27
flavours, of quarks, 37, 105, 108; in Jain particle physics, 37-38
forces; super, 102; energy, 10; in nature, 105; magnetic, 18; dynamic and stationary, 30, 32, 35, 37; fundamental 98, 105
Four Passions, *see* passions, four
freedom-longing catalyst, 11, 29
fusion, karmic, *see* karmic fusion

Gamow, G., 102
Gandhi, Mahatma 3, 4, 58
Gautama, Indrabhuti, 55, 119, 120
g-component, *see* longevity determining component
Glasenapp, von H., 50, 122
gluttony, 46-47
greed eliminated 65, 71, 76
subtle 65, 70, 76
suppressed, 65, 70, 76
gluon, 106
God, Jain arguments against 4, 17
go-mode, 34
Gosala, 118, 120

gravitation, force 10, 107
graviton 107
greed 46, 73, 75; degrees 50; one of the four passions, 46; in driving, 87, 89; in purification stages, 65, 69; time period, 50; *see* passions, the four
Gribbin, J. 102
Gross, gross-fine, gross-gross 36-37

Haldane, J.B.S., 99
Haribhadra, 123
Hawking, S.W., 109-10
h-component, *see* environmental determining component
heavenly stage, 25, 26; being, 26
Heisenberg, 109
hellish state, 25, 27; being, 26
helplessness, 82
Hemacandra, 123
higher vows, 69
holistic principle, 96, 101: analogy; elephant and the six blind men, 97, 98; science, 101
honey, 55
human, average, 21, 25, 40; state, 25-27
hydrogen atom, 104

insight-defiling component, 30; practical effect of 44; quality of true, 79-80; rarity of true 82; true, 66-69, 86
interaction of forces, 102; of karmic matter and soul, 10, 19, 33, 54, 76; of particles, 105

Jacobi, H., 60
Jahn, R.G., 102
Jain, C.R., 36
Jain G.R.., 102, 108
Jain, H.L. 119
Jain, N.L., 36
Jain, S.K., 107
Jain, Important dates in history of, 3, schools of, 5, 6; true path, 82
Jaini, J.L., 99, 114
Jaini, P.S., xi, 19, 27, 42, 51, 61, 81, 79, 124
jainism, characteristics of, 4-6; meaning of, 1
Jainness, 1, 64, 112
Jamali, 119
Jambo, 60
Jayadhavata, 122
jewels, the three *see* three jewels
Jina, 1, 6
Jinabhadra, 121
Jinasena, 122, 124
Jñānabāzi, 127

Kapashi, V., *ix*,
Karmagrantha, 122
karanānuyoga scripture, 123
karman-śarīra, 42
karmic agents, the five, 43, 67; body, bondage, 11, 13, 16; components, 14, 29, 30; computer, 63, 111; decay, 13-16, 19, 30, 45; density, 13; factors effecting karmic density, 14, 64, 65; fusion, *see* karmic fusion; influx, 11, 16, 66; matter, *see* karmic matter; field, 11, 46, 107; fission, 13, 15, 19, 66; force, 11, 15, 19, 29, 46, 107; force-field, 11, 43; particles, 10, 18, 35, process 11, 45; shield, 15, 19, 64, 82; total decay, 15, 82; twelve reflections, 82
karmic fusion, 7, 11, 13, 14, 19, 46, 79, 112; bosons, 107; dynamic medium, 35; and energy component, 30; karmic bondage, 7, 15, 48; karmic density, 14; nine reals, 15; passions, 45-46, 48, 49, 68-69; sthiti, 19; stopping of, 63; volitional activities, 43, 45-46, 51
karmic matter, 10, 14, , 19, 65; analogy: karmic matter as a virus, 18; analogy with gold, 9; analogy with petrol, 18; analogy with magnetism, 18; heavy/light, 7, 13, 53, 56; role in cycles, 33 karmons, 10, 36, 111-13; free state, 45; infinite in karmic matter, 36, 45
karmic reactor, 111-12

kaṣāyaprābhṛta, 124
kevalajñāna, of Mahāvīra, 119
King, U., xi
knowledge, 19, 29, 63; right (one of the three jewels), 4, 63, 85, 86; obscuring component, 30, 41, 44; of soul 10, 14, 19, 21, 37;
Kothari, D.S., 96
Kundakunda, 26, 124

layman, fifth stage of purification, 80,
leptons, 103
liberated state, 15; of soul, 19, 25, 26, 33
life-axis, 21-24, 29, 64; and karmic matter, 40, 55
life-units, 21, 23, 55; apples, 23; animal, 23; onion, 23, 55; plant, 23, 55
linear view, 94
literal view, 94
longevity determining karmic (g-) component, 30, 41, 45
lower vows, 70, 80, 81

magnetism, 36; force, 102, 105; analogy, 17, 18
Mahalanobis, P.C., 99
Mahāvīra, 5, 40, 55, 60; 24th tirthankara, 1-4; career as a tirthankara, 119; kevalajnana, 119; life of, 117; Mokṣa, 60, 120; relation to Gosala, 118; Sevetambara image, 2, 6
Mardia, K.V., 87, 98-99, 101
Marett, P., viii
masters, spiritual, 24-25, 70
mastery of afflictions, *see* afflictions, mastery of
Matilal, B.K., 99
matter, 35, 41; categories of, 36; characteristics of, 37; karmic, *see* karmic matter
meat, non-eating 55
media, dynamic and stationary, 34-35, 41, 102
meditation, 4, 79, 81, 83, 90; and spiritual progress, virtuous, 83
Meditation, mournful 8; wrathful 8
Mehta, B.K., 50
mental states, 25-26, 44-45, 85; reflections, 82
mesons, 103-104
micro-organisms, 23, 26, 54-55
mind, body and speech: karmic field, 46; limiting, 44; meditation, 85; restraint, 81, 83; violence/non-violence, 53, 57, volitional activities, 53, 63; yoga, 44
mind and matter, 44; restraint and, 81, swastika, 25, 26; as sixth sense, 38
mode, stop- and go-, 34
mokṣa and black hole, 38, 110; attainment, 69, 81, 84-85; chance of 61; liberation, 19; Mahāvīra, 60, 120; purification stages, 70; three jewels, 85; true insight, 82, 86
monks, practices, 81, 83; law book, 121

Nandighoshvijay, ix
naya, 93-94
neutrino, 36, 103, 109
neutron, 103-4, 106-107
nine reals, 15, 83, 93; subsidiary passions, 51, 71
Nirvana 4
non-obsolutism, 112
non-restraint, 43, 51, 64, 72
non-violence, 4, 56, 60, 64, 68-69 113
nuclear reactor, 63; weak and strong forces, 102

Nyayavatara, 124

odour in Jaina particle physics, 38; *see* also smell
omniscience, 93-94
onion, 23, 55, 112

palpability, 108-09
Pal, P., 127
Parsva, 23rd Tirthankara, 1, 6: Digambara image of, 5-6
particle karmic, *see* karmic particle; elementary, 99; passiono, 107;

ultimate, 35, 41
particle physics, 101; Jain, 38, 108
passiono, 107
passions, 43, 53, 64, 81; analogy: the four, 45-47, 51, 55, 66, 68, 71-72, 86; particle, 107; subsidiary, 51, 71-72, 84; and volitional activities, 45; *see* anger, deceit, greed, pride
Pauli's exclusion principle in a Jaina, 39, 109
Pavlov, 99
Pedler, K., 40
perception and attitude, 68; knowledge, 63; component, 30, 41, 44; perfect beings, 6, 17, 19, 25; perfection monks, 83; and righteousness, 81; of soul, 10, 19, 29, 37, 43, 63, 93; Tirthankaras, 58
personal karmic computer, 63, 111
plants, 22, 55
possessions, 81, 85, 113
Popper, K., 99
pratima (renunciation stages), 90
Pravacansāra, 124
predications, conditional, 86, 95, 101; degress, 50
pride, 46; in driving, 87, 89; in purification stages, 69; *see* passions, the four
Priyadarsana, 117, 119
proton, 103, 106, 113
purification stages, 64; analogy with production of ghee, 87; axis, 64, 65, fourth 69; fourteen, 64-65, 79; snakes and ladders, 127-128

quantum theory, 96, 101
quark, 103-04
quasipassions, 50, 51

random motion of karmons, 10
Rao, C.R., 9
Raychand, 4, 58
reals, nine, 15, 83, 86
reflective twelves, 82
reincarnation, 4, 32, 40, 42
religion, Jain, 1, 16, 38, 80; and science, 101, 109
renunciation, 86; eleven Model stages 80; Mahāvīra, 118; of nigoda ridden substances, 61; and righteousness, 81
restraint, 81, 83, 89; complete, 65, 89; rituals in temples, 6; the three, 81, 83, 89
righteousness, 79, 81, 90; ten rules, 81
Rsabha, 1, 7

Samadeva, 103
Samayasara, 124
sagarpomas, 59
Sanmatisutra, 124
Satkhaṇḍāgama, 124
Saxe J.G., 98, 113
science and religion, 101, 110
scriptures, 4, 7, 94, 121; Ācāradaśah, 122; Āvaśyaka, 123; Bhagavatī, 122; Caranānuyoga, 123; Dasavaikalika, 123, 126; Dravānuyoga, 123; Hindu, 119; Jain, 121; Kalpasutra, 60, 123; Karanānuyoga, 123; main, 121-122; Prathmānuyoga, 123; secondary, 123; Sūtrakṛtāṅga, 121; Tattvārthasūtra, 4, 8, 124, 125-26; Uttarādhyayana, 122, 126
Sermons, 121
Shah, A.R., 111
Shah, N. xi
Sheldrake, R., 109
Siddhartha, 117
Singhvi, L.M., 9
smell, sense of, 23, 37, 108; *see* also odour;
Snake and ladders, 127-28
Somadeva, 124
soul analogy with gold, 9; analogy with magnet, 17, 18; anlogy with petrol, 18; bliss 10, 44; composed of, 10; complete ignorance, 66; contaminated death, 29, 32, 70; degree of purity of, 9, 21; dynamic/stationary medium, 33-34; elements, 10, 14, 29, embodies, 10; Jain logic, 93; and karmic matter, 10-11, 13, 21, 29, 40-41, 43, 51, 53; liberated soul, 25, 37,

40; main properties of, 10, 37; nine reals, 15; one of the six existents, 33, 34; perfect, 17, 63, perception element, 68; *see* also perception, of soul; perverted, 67; polluted, 36; pure, *see* soul, perfect; purification stages; *see* purification stages reflections, 82; right faith, 85; salvation, 4; states of the, 13-15; violence, 56
space, 33-34, 41; occupied/unoccupied, 19, 33, 37; one of the six existents, 33
spiritual advancement, 25, 53, 84; blockage, 44; ladder, 40; master, 25; path, 1, 6, 25; purification, 64, 72, 82; teacher, 24, 25, 39, 70, 71 victor, 1
states dynamic omniscience, 70-71, 84; four mental states, 25-26, 85; liberated, 15-16, 25-26, 33, 37; long-term equilibrium, 14
stationary medium, 34, 41, 103
statistical thinking, 95
Stevenson, S., 46
sthiti, 19
stop-mode, 34
subsidiary passions, 51, 71, 84
Sudharman, 60, 121
Supersensory knowledge, 94
Svetambara, 5-6, 8; image of Mahavira, 2
swastika, 25, 86
syllogism: 86; Aristotelian, 95; Jain 94; medium, 94-95

taste, sense of 23
Tatia, N., 85, 93-94, 99
Tattvartha-sutra, 4, 8, 93, 123-124
teacher, spiritual, 25, 70-71
temporal cycle, 59
Three Jewels, 85-86, 90
time, to decay of karmic matter, 45; as the fouth dimension, 35, 109; as one of the six existents, 33, 35, 41; in Holistic principle, 98-99; sections, half cycles, 58
Tirthankara, 1-2, 5, 71; contact with other worlds, 60; living, 58; Mahavira, 1, 2, 119-20; Parsva, 1, 5, 6; Rsabha, 1, 7; stages of dynamic omniscience, 71; time-sections of, 60
Tobias M., 111, 114
tomato, 55
touch in Jain particle physics, 38, 108; sense of 22-23, 27, 38, 108
transatheism, 16
transportation, 29, 32
Trisala, 117
Truth tables, 96

ultimate particles, 35, 37; attributes of, 108; Jain particle physics, 38-40
Umasvati, 79, 85; Tattvartha-sutra, 4, 8, 93, 123-24
uncertainty, 95
uncertainty, principle of, 95, 109
universe, 34, 58, 82, 91, 101, 109 composed of, 9, 33; evolution, 17 Mahavira's contemplation of 118, six existents, 33
Upadhye, A.N., 119

Vardhamana, *see* Mahavira
vegetarianism 4, 55, 112; dead flesh 23, 55; figs 55; onion vs apples, 23, 55; roots, 22; tomato 55
violence, 4, 53-55, 57, 114; volitional aspect, 56; fusion 53
Virasena, 122
virtuous meditation, 83
Volition, uniformly mild, 69-70, 76; unprecedented 69-70, 76
volitional activities, 45, 53, 55-56, 63
vows, 80

watchfulness, 72, 79, 81, 89-90; five types, 81-89; in a driver, 89
water-bodies, 22, 27
Williams, R., 81
Wilson, 41
worry, 51, 85

Yasoda, wife of Mahavira, 117
Yasovijaya, 124
yoga, 43, 51, 76; positive, 44, 53; negative, 44, 53; Jain, 43, 85

Zaveri, J.S., 37, 108
zygote, 108